What Happens When Students Are in the Minority

Experiences That Impact Human Performance

EDITED BY
CHARLES B. HUTCHISON

ROWMAN & LITTLEFIELD EDUCATION
Lanham • New York • Toronto • Plymouth, UK

Published in the United States of America
by Rowman & Littlefield Education
A Division of Rowman & Littlefield Publishers, Inc.
A wholly owned subsidiary of The Rowman & Littlefield Publishing Group, Inc.
4501 Forbes Boulevard, Suite 200, Lanham, Maryland 20706
www.rowmaneducation.com

Estover Road
Plymouth PL6 7PY
United Kingdom

British Library Cataloguing in Publication Information Available

Library of Congress Cataloging-in-Publication Data

What happens when students are in the minority : experiences that impact human performance / [edited by] Charles B. Hutchison.
p. cm.
ISBN 978-1-60709-394-7 (cloth : alk. paper) — ISBN 978-1-60709-395-4 (pbk. : alk. paper) — ISBN 978-1-60709-396-1 (electronic)
1. Minorities—Education—United States—Case studies. 2. Minority students—United States—Social conditions—Case studies. I. Hutchison, Charles B.
LC3731.W48 2009
371.82900973—dc22 2009018072

∞™ The paper used in this publication meets the minimum requirements of American National Standard for Information Sciences—Permanence of Paper for Printed Library Materials, ANSI/NISO Z39.48-1992.
Manufactured in the United States of America.

To all who toil to transcend the effects
of their minority experiences
but find no pens to tell their stories,
and those who beat their swords into ploughshares
and add value to living

Contents

Preface

One of the perennial curiosities of life concerns the nature of human nature. As a student of human behavior, I have learned that when people congregate, they often unwittingly brandish the sword of discrimination, using any conceivable point of difference. This *difference* becomes a silent sword that can wound deeply, even if the sword is left untouched. Oftentimes, without doing a thing, without lifting a finger, those in the majority aim this sword at others—the minority—who are often acutely aware of this sword and its sharpness. Oftentimes, they are wounded just by being in the presence of this unwielded sword. When the majority, however, becomes conscious of its invisible sword, it can decide to put it back into its scabbard, and place it away. This creates a "sword-less" community where all humanity can live at ease and put their shoulders to the wheel.

Although this book was written using the narratives of educators in different life settings and has an educational orientation, it explains a general human phenomenon. For this reason, a good alternative title could have been "Humanity and the Minority Experience: Behaviors That Impact Performance" to speak to those who want to understand humans more deeply. Therefore, readers are encouraged to make the necessary extrapolations to foster a better human understanding and advance humanity.

In order to protect the identities of any parties and institutions mentioned in the narratives, pseudonyms have been used.

I

INTRODUCTION TO THE MINORITY EFFECT

Introduction

The "Minority Effect" as a Human Phenomenon and Its Educational Implications

CHARLES B. HUTCHISON

I thought to myself that the scream of the newborn has something of a question in it. It was a signal sent out by the newcomer to see if he had arrived at the right place. The sound most similar to a newborn's scream is the sound of children, which is why children in my village are required to cry out in confirmation of the newborn's arrival. This confirmation satisfies something in the psyche of the newborn, who is now ready to surrender to being present in this world. I have often wondered, what would happen to the newborn if there were no answer? Can infants recover from the damage done to their souls as a result of a message at birth that they are on their own? (Malidoma Somé, 1998, p. 93)

Consider the following true exchange between two educators in a course on diversity:

> *Teacher A:* I was just thinking about one of the next assignments we are going to do [attending a function of a racially and culturally different population], and . . . I realized that I had not been in an African American church by myself . . . because it will be the most out of my comfort zone. I don't know why. I think I will feel out of place [because] I may be the only white person there. I don't

know what they will think of me . . . I was thinking, "Hmm, I wonder who can go with me?" And then I thought, "I wonder if that is how some of my [minority] students feel all the time?"

Teacher B: Great points [Teacher A]! You said exactly what I was thinking, too, wondering who I could get to go [to a minority church] with me, [and] would I feel so out of place? That sort of thing. I hadn't thought about my students feeling that way. What a true suggestion!

The following conversation ensued between a mother and her daughter, Jamie. Jamie's father had just got a promotion on his job and moved to a new town. After serious research, they bought a house in a "good school district" in order to give Jamie and her siblings a good education. Unlike the previous school where Jamie was popular and well liked, Jamie and her siblings are now minorities in their new school:

Mother: Jamie, what is wrong? Why don't you want to go to school?

Jamie: I don't know. I don't like my new school.

Mother: But you liked your last school, and you like learning. . . .

Jamie: Yes, I like learning stuff, but my last school was different.

Mother: But how can you tell me that you like learning but don't want to go to school?

The last conversation ensued between a father and his son's teacher in the third week of school:

Teacher: Since the beginning of the semester, Johann has been engaging in some behaviors that concern me. How does he relate to others at home?

Father: This is surprising news to me. He is generally well behaved at home and plays very well with the kids in the neighborhood. He is new to this school, and I have been wondering if he has made any friends; he is not enthusiastic about coming to school.

Teacher: That is interesting because, in the last couple of weeks, he has been fighting with the other students and has been disruptive in class. He tries to threaten students whom he perceives as looking at him differently, and acts disrespectfully, not only toward them but to his teachers as well.

> *PAUSE FOR REFLECTION*
>
> What do you think was going on with these teachers and students? Were their feelings justifiable? Explain your reasoning.

REFLECTING ON THE MINORITY EXPERIENCE

Given the opportunity for reflection, most people would readily acknowledge that it is tough to be the obvious minority in any situation, even for adults. Surprisingly, however, the detrimental consequence of being the obvious minority in the school or social context has not gained the publicity it deserves. For this reason, it is easy to overlook minority students' complicated classroom experiences and the impact of such experiences on student learning. Since education is the gateway to students' future, this topic has an impact on students' future economic, mental, and social welfare.

Think about a simple question: Why is Sunday claimed to be the most racially segregated day in the United States? How is this phenomenon related to social dynamics in schools? Since schools are a mirror of the society—for better or for worse—it is common to find students segregated into racial groups. Beverly Tatum's (1997) book *Why Are All the Black Kids Sitting Together at the Cafeteria?* captures this phenomenon in the school setting.

> *PAUSE FOR REFLECTION*
>
> Think about a time when you found yourself in a situation where you realized that you were the only minority (e.g., the only male, female, religious, or racial minority), and you could not escape. How did you feel? If you were given a test at that time—or just asked to stand up and say a few words—how well would you have performed? The concept of *stereotype threat* partly explains this phenomenon.

STEREOTYPE THREAT AND THE MINORITY

The social psychologist Claude Steele (1999) described a form of anxiety called *stereotype threat*. He explained that stereotype threat is related to conventional anxiety, whereby people who are conscious of their tense social situation may become distracted, experience an increase in body temperature, and suffer diminished performance levels. Long before Steele's idea of stereotype threat was conceived, social scientists and cognitive psychologists had identified social anxiety as a source of identity and academic challenge for certain populations. For example, in 1978, Simmons, Brown, Bush, and Blyth indicated that differences in academic achievements between black and white students were related to their self-esteem. In a similar vein, Saenz (1994) had revealed that the extra *cognitive burden* due to one's *minority status* had significant detrimental effects on one's academic performance.

During stereotype threat, one is likely to underperform in a manner consistent with preconceived stereotypes; a kind of self-fulfilling prophecy. Steele attributes this kind of underperformance to a person's anxiety of conforming to negative stereotypes and investing emotional energy so as to overcome them. Apparently, this obsession with self-presentation overburdens one's cognitive machinery. Therefore, people in the minority who are conscious of their status do not perform to their full potential.

THE CONSCIOUS "OTHER" AS THE MINORITY

PAUSE FOR REFLECTION

Why do many musical performers feel compelled to use alcohol or other mind-altering substances during their performances? What do the mind-altering substances do for them? In what ways does this relate to the minority's experience?

Being the "other" is a natural human phenomenon, and there are several factors that can bring about the experience of being the *other* or the minority in a given situation. These include race, religion, sex, gender, income status, familiarity with a topic, and other characteristics. Because most people are likely to find themselves as minorities in specific contents, it is easier to think of individuals in these circumstances as *situational minorities.* In the school context, there are many situations whereby students from both the majority and minority racial populations find themselves as the minorities in the school or the classroom. For example, although racial minorities are generally the "other" in schools and classrooms, it is common to find whites who are the minorities in large urban schools. In many schools where there are large percentages of all races, racial minority students often find themselves as the minorities in advanced courses, for several reasons. One basic reason, however, is that many try to avoid being the only minorities in such classes, even if they are capable of succeeding in them.

The notion of *consciousness* is vital in the discussion about minorities, since it determines the level of comfort one experiences as the minority in a given situation. Delia Saenz's (1994) work indicates that *tokenization* is an important aspect of the minority experience. In other words, individuals need to be aware that they are indeed the token individuals (or that they are different, for any reason) in a given situation in order for them to feel the burden thereof—for example, the only white on the mostly black basketball team, the only black in the orchestra, the only female on a team or in the classroom, or the student or worker who is somehow aware that his or her performance is connected to his or her race, gender, or some identifiable factor. For this reason, Osborne (2001) noted that stereotype threat is a wider human phenomenon that probably exists in many areas of life, including business and industry.

STEREOTYPE THREAT, CONFIDENCE, AND COMFORT

> *PAUSE FOR REFLECTION*
>
> Imagine being blindfolded and being placed on an unfamiliar roller coaster. How would you feel about the ride? What if you decided to ride on the same roller coaster again, with your eyes open? What accounts for the differences in experience? How would you describe your experience after having tried the same ride about twenty times? Again, what accounts for the differences in experience?

The effect of stereotype threat can be complicated or even diluted by one's level of *confidence* or *comfort*. As will be obvious in the narratives in this book, participants of the Minority Experience exercise (explained later) were very anxious, especially if this experience was the first of its kind for them. This is similar to a first-time roller coaster ride. In some instances in this book, however, the authors indicated that they were relatively more comfortable than they otherwise would have been because they were used to people of other races or that they were used to being the *other* (e.g., Matt Reid). This is similar to a multiple-time roller coaster ride. In fact, some of the participants even went to the extent of putting themselves in the situation where they would experience the fuller effect of the *minority experience,* such as sitting toward the front of the congregation, where they would be more visible. In such situations, the "threat" of the unknown is diminished to some degree, although the awareness of one's tokenism remains.

There are other situations where certain people may enjoy their minority status—although that still does not negate their token status. Let us think about two examples: In the first example, think about the international student who once traveled to a small, remote town in Hungary, where no one had ever physically met a dark African. Being a confident, gregarious person, this student felt like a pop star, "one of a kind." Take another scenario where a white person traveled to a remote Asian village where the children had never met a white person. The personal outcomes for both individuals were the same: In both cases, the visitors not only felt special but also encountered warm, welcoming groups of people. The result was a feeling of comfort and a sense of self-confidence.

Although being the minority within the larger school setting may have some social implications, this book is concerned with minorities' experiences in the context of the classroom and their learning experiences.

PURPOSE OF AND HOW TO READ THIS BOOK

If you have read this book to this point, then you deserve to know how this book is organized. The purpose of this book is twofold: (1) to introduce selected real-life experiences of practicing and prospective educators who became the "conscious minorities" in specific contexts, and (2) to discuss the behavioral patterns hereby termed *the minority effect.* These behaviors emerge from over 150 students' observations and discussions as they engaged in an exercise termed "Experiencing the Minority," over several semesters (the instructions for this activity are provided in the box entitled "Activity and Reflection: Experiencing the Minority"). The primary objective of this exercise was to help educators to arrive at a personalized understanding of the educational implications of being the minority in the learning environment. For this reason, the essays in this book emphasize connections for helping students of any race who constitute the minorities in any school environment.

This book is divided into five parts for specific reasons. Identity development studies, including the works of William Cross (e.g., 1978), indicate that mainstream minority students have no other option than to integrate into the large society in order to be successful. This process involves relationships with the majority group, a process that results in racial self-consciousness or minority identity development. Cross's work may generally help minority teachers to understand themselves in terms of their racial identity development. Janet Helms's (1984) research, however, is useful for helping racial majority teachers to understand themselves in terms of their racial identity development. It indicates that the majority population has the *majority prerogative*: the option to engage or disengage in the minority experience.

Whereas Part I introduces the basic concepts for understanding the contents of the book, Part II presents racially different minority educators' narratives. This grouping is important because minority individuals are generally more familiar with the minority experience, and that comes through in their narratives. Readers are encouraged to read between the lines and analyze the psychological frameworks from which these educators emerge. In Part III, white educators' experiences are featured. In general, fewer white educators will be found to have previously experienced the minority effect owing to the fact that they belong to the majority group and are therefore less likely to be in a racial minority's position. When they faced situations where being the minority would have resulted in their discomfort, they had the option of exercising their majority prerogative and avoiding them. For this reason, it is helpful for readers to examine how the majority prerogative shaped their experiences. Part IV provides short narratives that complement those in Parts II and III, and Part V provides a thematic summary of the lessons or concepts learned from the whole book (last chapter), besides narratives that address the needs of readers who seek direct applications in the classroom (Ann Wright's work) or relatively more theoretical ideas (Jones's, Clark's, and Afam's works).

ACTIVITY AND REFLECTION: EXPERIENCING THE MINORITY

The purpose of this exercise is to (1) understand other cultures and (2) experience, as closely as possible, what your minority students experience and feel in your or other teachers' classes, and what you can do about it.

- Visit a congregation (or any race-based formal gathering place, such as synagogue, mosque, or festival) of a race other than your own. For example, if you are a white teacher in a predominantly minority school, visit a church for the

(*continued*)

ethnic group most represented in your school (e.g., Latino or black.) On the other hand, if you are a minority teacher in a predominantly white school, although you somewhat understand the feelings involved, still visit a white congregation—just to be more conscious of this phenomenon.

- It is recommended that you go alone, and to a smaller congregation, in order to approximate the feelings minority students are likely to experience in a normal classroom.
- While there, if possible, attempt to engage with the members—and note the experience.
- As soon as the meeting is over, answer the following questions:
  - In what ways does this experience relate to the cultural elements of this group of people? (Think about talking, singing, sound levels, preaching style, visuals, movement, etc.)
  - How did you feel being the minority in the room?
  - How successful were you in engaging with the members of the congregation?
  - How many were you able to *heartily* connect with?
  - How cordial did they appear to be with each other, as compared to you?
  - Were there any surprises?
  - Based on your experience, how do you think your minority students (of any race) feel in your classroom?
  - In what ways can you help your minority students to be more comfortable in your classroom and your school?

"ACTING THE MINORITY" IN THE CLASSROOM: THE MINORITY EFFECT

In my courses, one of the interesting observations students have made is that, related to the phenomenon of *acting white* (whereby some minority students refrain from acting in ways identifiable with the white culture), there is a pervasive phenomenon that may be called *acting the minority* or *the minority effect.* In this phenomenon, minority students (i.e., the significantly few students from a different ethnic group in a predominantly black, white, or Latino class) generally sit in the back of the classroom and often slump in their chairs as if to hide themselves, and they will not take the initiative to participate in class discussions. Arguably (as evident from the narratives in this book), such students are making conscious efforts to become invisible in the group. By sitting in the back of the class, they escape the visual field of most observers. In some cases, the students would sit close to the door as if they are ready to escape the discomforts of the class if they could. Moreover, by slumping (or attempting to fold over) in their chairs, they are inadvertently trying to physically shrink their bodies in order to become less visible.

THE ACADEMIC CONSEQUENCE OF THE MINORITY EFFECT

In psychological terms, one may argue that acting the minority is a physical expression of an unconscious experience, one whereby tokenized individuals are trying to vanish from their classrooms. Of course, people who are attempting to vanish in class would not volunteer to speak, since they are already self-conscious and are trying to avoid any attention. Logically, this lack of class participation makes them susceptible to lower academic performance, since they do not get the opportunity to test their misconceptions or other ideas for correction or refinement, leading to academic disadvantage. For minority students in predominantly white schools, this phenomenon may feed into the stereotype of minority failure. When white students constitute the minority in a racial minority school or classroom, they, too, are widely observed exhibiting this behavior—as also evident in whites' narratives in this book. Therefore, this phenomenon is pervasive cross-culturally.

EXPERIENCING DIFFERENCES

When students engage in the Experiencing the Minority exercise, many report that this is one of the toughest psychological exercises they have done thus far in their whole educational experience. During this exercise, they generally report that they feel extremely self-conscious. Some have even described their feelings as "sticking out like a sore thumb," especially my white students who may have had the prerogative of avoiding minority cultures throughout their lives and still become successful in United States. Related to the theme of self-consciousness, another common theme reported by students was the feeling of heightened awareness of their surroundings. Students generally noted that they were acutely aware of *differences.* If they visited a church for the exercise, many were extremely conscious of the fact that they were not familiar with the new church's rituals, song lyrics, melodies, or even the sequences by which the different congregations sang otherwise familiar songs. These different singing traditions led them to make "mistakes" when singing songs they thought they already knew. Therefore, in the proverbial axiom of "adding insult to injury," they felt like people who were "sticking out like sore thumbs" and making mistakes on top of that, with the "whole world watching."

Another notable observation is that students from different racial groups who had had more meaningful previous relationships with people from the other races were likely to feel relatively more at ease than those who were insulated from them.

EXPERIENCING THE MINORITY: A TOUGH EXPERIENCE

In general, Experiencing the Minority is a tough exercise for all my students. For some, even though they are willing—or rather obligated—to endure this exercise, they psychologically prime themselves for the day, expecting that it would be mentally taxing on them. Others try clever means of avoiding the true impact of the exercise by visiting with their friends, spouses, or other family members (as is evident from Students A and B in the introduction) or visiting the church of a teacher-colleague from a different race. Some attend large, "predominantly" black or white congregations where they know that it is more likely to find others of their race so that they are not alone in this experience. Interestingly, some of the students reported that when they were the minority in the church, they were seated close to members of their racial group—an assumption of the church ushers that, somehow, this would be of some psychological benefit (comfort) to them. Ironically, when other token minorities are present in the congregation, much as there is a mutual curiosity about the other, there is also a level of avoidance of each other—possibly an attempt to "silence" attention to themselves. All these actions constitute obvious attempts at seeking comfort, by any means possible. A few of my students were not able to "endure" the full experience and chose not to complete the exercise, owing to the level of discomfort they felt.

THE NATURAL QUEST FOR COMFORT: A BASIC HUMAN NEED

From these observations, it is obvious that my student participants are in a quest for comfort. This comfort is partly achieved by creating a "comfort zone" or a "circle of comfortable people" around themselves—by surrounding themselves with family, friends, or people who look like them.

Discomfort is a serious but basic human experience. People would do anything possible to avoid it, even at some cost. In the experiences above, the participants have generally been adults in a postbaccalaureate program. The pertinent questions therefore are: (1) If even adults cannot handle being the minorities in any given situation, how much more growing adolescents? (2) What are the costs of being the minority in any situation, especially in the learning environment? (3) What can educators do to mitigate such experiences?

COMPENSATING FOR THE MINORITY EFFECT

Similar to adults' experiences, when adolescents find themselves in the situation whereby they are confined in spaces where they are the minorities, they find ways to compensate for their feelings. For some students, the simple but sad solution is to avoid (the generally advanced) classes normally populated by white students, or simply avoid schools where they would become the minorities. One way to avoid such advanced classes is to fare poorly in school (or avoid "acting white"). This contributes to racially segregated schooling in desegregated schools and the achievement gap issue, whereby minority students fare worse academically than majority students.

Whereas some minority students may retreat into silence and passive classroom existence, others may feel that they are visible, anyway, and therefore find more visible ways to direct attention *away* from themselves. For this latter group, the response could potentially be negative, reminiscent of Steele's phenomenon of stereotype threat. Teachers generally report that these students may, for instance, become the class clowns. Instead of focusing their cognitive resources on classroom instruction, these students would rather use them to think about ways to entertain the class, thus costing them in academic performance. In the end, by trying to neutralize their minority presence in class, these adolescents would have come full circle to fulfilling the academically unsuccessful minority stereotype.

SOLUTIONS

There are many means by which humans can achieve comfort, an antidote to the minority effect. What can be learned from students' Experiencing the Minority narratives is that familiarity breeds comfort. When family and friends were around, they were comfortable. This may translate as physical comfort. From the narratives, psychological comfort was also evident. When the participants were able to connect with the familiar—be they a familiar hymn, ritual, or even someone they had previously seen in their communities—they achieved some sense of comfort. These observations have some classroom implications for diversity-conscious instructors. Consider the following student excerpts:

> *Student A:* When I was attending a university in the South, I was the only white person in the "Introduction to African American Studies" course, and the experience was very interesting. I was very worried at first that I would not fit in, but the instructor told me that he was glad that I was in the class and that he would love to hear my perspective of things during conversations. I had a blast in the class; the room was always lively with discussions on the issues about which we read for our homework, and my classmates were not afraid to speak their mind. I had never seen African Americans so outspoken before. In all my other classes where African Americans were the minority, they would mostly keep to themselves or not talk at all. The contrast in behavior was amazing from a majority white standpoint.
>
> *Student B:* My classroom consists of about twenty white students, ten African American students, three Hispanic students, and two Asian students. I try to create diverse groups when we do class [group] work. If I do not choose the groups for them, many times they will huddle together into racially segregated groups. [As my intervention,] I chose the groups at the beginning of the year, [and] they fought me. . . . Now they seem to flock toward the same students they have been in groups with before, no matter their race. They can and do learn about other students' backgrounds, which is just as important as chemistry.

These excerpts indicate that (1) students exhibit their highest potentials when in comfortable environments, and (2) teachers need to intervene in behalf of both their minority and majority students so that while the minority students may benefit from increased comfort levels for better learning outcomes, the majority students may benefit from broader, cross-cultural understanding that is needed to survive in an increasingly multicultural, global society.

It has been proposed in the earlier sections that humans are likely to use their physical and psychological resources to achieve comfort. If they realize that comfort could potentially evade them, they would find all sorts of means to regain it. This is no different in the classroom since adolescent students would find both positive and negative means to achieve comfort. However, it is possible for teachers to create this sought-after comfort zone in several ways. Including the following:

- Understanding the nature of the minority effect as a psychological phenomenon and its implications in the classroom
- Talking to the students, identifying their backgrounds, and introducing familiar objects in the classroom environment (i.e., make the classroom psychologically homelike)
- Fostering cross-cultural understanding and actively nurturing cross-cultural collaboration (such as the diverse grouping in Student B's excerpt; this excerpt indicated that familiarity—even interracial ones—fosters comfort)
- Actively seeking to make minority students comfortable and feeling welcome in class; this could take the form of (1) fostering natural friendships in class for such students, (2) using effective cooperative grouping dynamics to bring out the strengths of all students, (3) bundling the minority students together in specific classes to minimize the "minority effect," and (4) preferential seating of students for both comfort and inclusion.

CONCLUSION

One of the most important but limited factors in the classroom is students' attention. Oftentimes, what makes students attend in class is the absence of distractions. Student attention and apparent student interest go hand in hand. When the minority effect is minimized, student experiences are likely to change for the better. Concurrently, students are more likely to reallocate more of their cognitive resources to attend in class, thereby precipitating greater success in school.

In conclusion, teachers should fully question the conventional explanations for the nature of minority student interest and academic disengagement, and wonder how such academic pathologies may potentially be symptomatic of students' awareness of their psychological subjugation within a majority classroom culture. Subsequently, teachers should take measures to actively invite and include minority students in class work.

SUMMARY

When students comprise the minority in the classroom context, they tend to exhibit certain predictable behaviors. These may include attempts at being less visible through diminishing one's presence, avoiding engagement, and using compensatory mechanisms for deflecting attention from themselves. These behavior patterns are hereby termed *the minority effect*, and they have negative impacts on student learning. Teachers therefore need to be aware of such students' needs and find ways to make them a seamless and integral part of the class.

Please see the end of the final chapter for some discussion questions.

II

THE MINORITY EXPERIENCE FROM THE PERSPECTIVE OF RACIAL MINORITIES

1

My Dark Curly Thick Hair Was a Nemesis as All I Wanted Was the Blond Straight Hair Parted Down the Middle, *and* Romeo: A Misunderstood Student

ANITA MCGEE

THE OUTSIDER LOOKING IN

The world is a much scarier place, especially if you feel that you are an outsider looking in. That was how I felt when I was in fifth grade. Enrolled in an upper-middle-class school, my name was a beacon for the minority label. Anita Marie Sanchez was the perpetual red flag among the typical American names like Sally Jones, Jim Wentworth, and Debbie English. My dark curly thick hair was a nemesis as all I wanted was the blond straight hair parted down the middle, which all the other girls had. Every school day was a reminder of what I was *not.* Not only did I look the part of my family's lower socioeconomic status, but I was also *not* what the rest of my classmates were. We had a residence in Newport, Rhode Island—a small townhome—while we were on a waiting list for military housing. The prominent upper-income families and the rich lived on the small Eight-Mile Island, home to Cliff Walk mansions and Americas Cup races.

Consequences of an Outsider Looking In

I was an outsider looking in, and certainly not part of the majority group. To accentuate this situation was the name-calling, the group intimidating threats, isolation, and the low expectations from the teachers. Needless to say, I felt neglected, abused, and somewhat ashamed. I was helpless, I now see, because the situation was beyond my control. I could not control their actions toward me any more than I had the ability to change who I was. I responded to the situation the only way I knew how: with my sharp words and my fists. At the time, it seemed to be the best way to handle the situation, much to my parents' chagrin. Now, I realize that perhaps I should have used a more diplomatic method of solving my problems, but these are merely empty words to a frightened and angry nine-year-old.

My actions resulted in not only short-term but also long-term consequences. My actions only perpetuated the stereotypes the other children had made about me. The teachers' fears about my disposition were maddeningly confirmed because I had resorted to violence, which only resulted in my feelings of increased isolation. My parents suffered as well as a result: they were never able to become good friends with their neighbors or others in the community because they had to defend me. I remember one such occasion when one of our neighbors came knocking at our door because I had bloodied their son's nose, and my parents were my first and only line of defense against their accusations.

Fortunately for me, I was able to move away from Rhode Island after five years because my father was in the military and was transferred to a place where I was not discriminated against. However, I realize that not everyone has a chance to escape from the problems that surround them.

Looking in the Mirror

For many years, I had problems accepting who I was because of the way I looked. I truly didn't like what I saw when I looked in the mirror—years of taunting and harassment haunted me through the glass. Not only was my own body image affected, but so was the way I formed relationships with others. It was extremely difficult for me to form healthy relationships with people even after I had moved away from Rhode Island. Even to this day, I still have problems trusting people, and it truly takes a great deal of time until I can assimilate them into my comfort zone.

Notwithstanding my challenging, minority-related experiences, I can see some positive sides. One moderately decent consequence of my minority experiences is that I have learned to better cope and adapt to any given situation. I find it easier, because of the fact I moved so many times as a child, and so I am always forced to become accustomed to my surroundings and the people in them. For this I am grateful, because it has served me well in life. I find that in my adult life, I am an advocate for bullied children. What I went through makes it impossible to turn a blind eye.

ROMEO: A MISUNDERSTOOD STUDENT

I met Romeo my first year as a teacher's assistant in a predominately white upper-middle-class elementary school. He caught my attention the very first day of his enrolment into fourth grade with his large physique and very dark skin color. In the days that followed, I noticed that he was having a very difficult time adjusting and relating to his peers—indeed, many expressed fear of his dominating presence. I sought out background information on Romeo, looking for ways to help him adjust. I learned that his family was struggling on many levels, including financially.

A Disposable, Gifted Child?

As a means of reaching out to Romeo, I requested to be his tutor in the math class he was first placed in. After working with him one-on-one successfully for two weeks, the math teacher had him switched to a lower-level class, and when I inquired as to why this action was taken, the response was "It was taking up too much of my time and hers." Needless to say, I was disappointed and felt she had low expectations of his abilities from the first week. This was not the first or last time Romeo was to have a teacher who had low expectations of his abilities. Fortunately, his homeroom teacher was forming some connections with him and felt he should be tested for attention deficit disorder (ADD). This resulted in a solution to one problem, but there were several others yet to conquer.

The next quandary to address was that of communication. When Romeo spoke, it was always in a loud, assertive, and combative tone. He never looked me directly in the eye unless he was specifically asked to do so, and even then it was clear to see that he was uncomfortable. After he was given medication for his previously addressed condition, he became more subdued and, I am sad to say, almost unresponsive.

Thus far, each teacher Romeo had had at this school was a white female. It appears to me that when Romeo appeared combative—and a misfit within the white school environment—they were unwilling to deal with his behavioral issues. However, when he was given medication, it seems as though he was never encouraged to achieve at the level I know him to be capable of. When Romeo and I worked in one-on-one situations, it was clear that he had an extensive knowledge of the subject matter at hand. He was especially interested in all things to do with dinosaurs; he was able to recite their scientific names and characteristics from memory.

It seems as though Romeo was an unfortunate child who was unfairly treated and cheated by the "system." The last I heard of him was that he had graduated from the fifth grade and was living in a homeless shelter. His homeroom teacher and I were very concerned that he would not receive the services he so desperately needed, and the last teacher he had was abrasive and very devoid of nurturing. It is my hope he will encounter educators who will foster his desire to learn and truly see his abilities for what they are. Romeo needs a sense of belonging.

TEACHING REFLECTIONS

Having observed a minority group in a setting outside school, reflecting on my own experiences as an outsider, and witnessing the process of being a minority from a student's point of view, how, then, are the minority students in *my* classroom affected? During the first week of school, my students asked many questions pertaining to my background, my marital status, and my own children. One of my students directly asked me whether I was Hispanic; it was clear they were not only attempting to connect with me but also classify me. My students at this school are extremely diverse; the majority group is the African American population, followed by Latinos, and finally Asians. However, diverse as this group is, they all share a passionate curiosity about who I am.

I began my first weeks at my new school by introducing my students to various artists. They were enthralled by personal stories of Frida Kahlo and Vincent Van Gogh and seemed, at an almost subconscious level, to connect with these masters of the paintbrush. Both Kahlo and Van Gogh had to overcome tremendous adversity to be successful; Kahlo survived after having been hit by a bus and lived in excruciating pain, and Van Gogh was forced to live a life tainted by mental illness and ridiculed for his paintings. My students were drawn to these characters and their lives—an insight that encouraged me to present them with other "food for thought."

My students were also extremely interested in any activity in which they could become physically involved. They were not just content to listen to artistic theory and see me demonstrate the correct way to draw a line; instead, they wanted to physically participate. Rather than having them draw the lines, they, using their bodies, *became* the lines. My classroom was dotted with horizontal, vertical, and even diagonal children who enjoyed every minute of the lesson.

This is a new class and a new setting for me, and I have been struggling with the noise level and students who speak while I am speaking. It has been frustrating, and I have relayed that frustration to the students. However, after this minority experience, I know that, culturally they are accustomed to a higher noise level than me; it is part of who they are. To become an effective teacher, I am learning more about my students' cultural backgrounds.

If I could change my classroom in any way, I would change the way in which my students respond to one another. The boys especially seem so angry to the point of puffing out their chests and spouting fighting words at the target of their perceived unhappiness. Rational talks and defusing strategies sometimes do not provide the desired outcome. And then I remember a very angry girl of nine.

2

Black and Female in an All-White and Male Math Class, *and* Mercy's Dilemma

ORA UHURU

When in college, I needed to take a math course in a nearby college, since that course was not offered at my school. This was a predominantly white college. The instructor was a white male, and the students in the math class were 98 percent white males and 2 percent female: I was one of the females, and the other one was white.

On the first day of class, we were given the syllabus of all the course assignments with the due date for each assignment. I considered myself to be a very studious student who was hardworking and determined to be successful. In this class, however, I felt isolated and lonely. The fact that I was in the minority in both race and gender compounded the situation. I thought that I at least had a connection with the other female in the class, but not for long; for some reason, she dropped the class after about two weeks, making matters worse, and I was left alone to face a white-male-dominated audience. I knew then that I had some decisions to make—and had just a short time to make them. Upon thinking about it, I knew that because of my upbringing, dropping the class was out of the question. I decided to stay in the class and do my best—which was not going to be good enough.

First of all, I had a very difficult time understanding the instructor because of his deep regional accent. Lucky for me, he wrote all of his notes on the board, and that made it easier for me to understand the contents. Second, although my instructor was as supportive as he could be of the only female in a class among a group of young white men, the one thing that I will always remember is that each time I made a mistake, the entire class would snicker or make little sarcastic remarks. The instructor, as fair as I thought he was, never bothered to address the young men or deter this behavior. This was humiliating, to say the least. I felt so lonely and ashamed. Because the teacher failed to address the students' remarks, I wondered if he was in agreement with their comments.

Most normal people would have just dropped out of the course, but I *refused* to give them the satisfaction. I did not want to stereotype my race or myself by giving up. So I did the next best thing: I asked one of my best friends who was a math major to tutor me. I wanted to shine and stand out among the rest of the students. In order to do this, I had to know everything before class started so I could just follow my teacher's lectures for reinforcement.

Before I asked my best friend to tutor me, I had made a couple of low grades on the tests in the course, so in order to survive the humiliation, I dug deep inside myself and convinced myself that these young men were no smarter or better than me. This took a lot of courage and willpower. After convincing myself that I was just as good, or better, than my course counterparts, I began to study really hard for clarity and understanding. My best friend was truly there for me. She went over every problem and situation one step at a time until I was comfortable. On the next test, I made a better score—a good start! I continued to study and virtually spent all my free time working on math problems. My next test scores were much better, which really boosted my confidence. My focus now changed from just doing well in this course to "plain old getting even"—and that is the one thing that kept me going. I was never angry; I just wanted to get even.

For the entire semester, I just studied, just to get even, and I completed the course with a B. Had it not been for the outside support I received from my best friend and others, I would have given up. It took a lot of energy on my part just to walk into this class, not to mention the hostile atmosphere that surrounded me, but at the time, I felt that I had no choice. I needed to do what I had to do so I could do what I wanted to do: graduate from college in three-and-a-half years.

My experience in this course and my accomplishment did a lot to help build my self-confidence. I know that there are not many students today who would subject themselves to this type of ordeal—and indeed, nobody should be forced to endure such hostile environments just to get an education. Having said that, I understand how students feel when placed in situations in which they feel inadequate, degraded, humiliated, and lonely. Most students today will not tolerate this type of atmosphere—and in my classes no student will ever have to tolerate that!

MERCY'S DILEMMA

One of my relatives, Mercy, was the only minority student at a predominantly white school. Mercy was excited about attending this school because it is considered prestigious. She was particularly overjoyed because she had been given a full scholarship to attend this school. Her parents' only responsibility was to make sure that she arrived at school on time each day.

Each day, Mercy would wake up and hurriedly dress so she would be on time. She was always excited about attending this school especially since she was the only one in her class accepted to attend the school. She made a commitment to herself that she would be the best at every activity in which she was a participant.

Back to the Beginning

On the first day of class, Mercy arrived on time and entered the building. She went to her academic adviser to pick up her class schedule. The academic adviser was very cordial, greeted her with a big smile, and escorted her to her first morning class. However, Mercy did not realize that the students who normally escort new students around the campus had refused to do this for her. She entered her class and sat in a seat at the front, close to the window—she was from a rural area and especially liked nature, and so she wanted to be have a view of the outdoors. As the students entered and began to settle down, the teacher asked each one to stand and introduce him- or herself, including a little background information. When it was Mercy's turn, she rose, stated her name and where she was from, but there were some giggles. As the day wore on, she noticed that most of other students avoided her. She was a little naive and thought nothing about these incidents.

Mercy tried to engage her classmates, but when she spoke to them, she did not get clear responses, so she decided not to talk to any student who did not want to talk to her. By this time, she was only talking to her teacher because most of the students would not engage with her in conversation. After about a week of this type of treatment from her peers, she questioned whether she had made the right choice coming to this school. Because of the treatment she received from her peers, she refused to participate in extracurricular activities. She had no trouble inside the classroom because she was a very bright student. It appeared, however, that the better her grades were in the class, the less likely her peers would associate with her on the playground.

Mercy was only in the eighth grade, and during this time in adolescents' life, they usually have other concerns in life. I could see that she was becoming withdrawn and less outgoing than when she first arrived. Her teacher also made the same observation. Although she felt that she was in no position to intervene in the situation with her other students, she decided to allow Mercy to do things in a less orthodox way: since she did not want to place Mercy in compromising situations, she allowed her to have extra library time to read, work on projects, and watch documentaries that related to people of her culture or ethnicity.

Saved by Her Brain

Earlier that school year, all eighth graders had to take the SAT examinations, and when the scores were released, it was discovered that Mercy had scored the highest in the entire county. The principal of the school did not let this accomplishment go unrewarded. He acknowledged her accomplishments over the intercom during morning announcements. She was congratulated by all of the teachers and only a few of her peers. But because she was very intelligent and exceptionally smart, many of her peers began associating with her, if for no other reason than to be viewed in a different light and possibly figure out how she could be so gifted.

This was a defining moment for Mercy, as she began to participate in many extracurricular activities, especially softball. It appeared that she was beginning to be accepted by most of her peers as well as people in the school community.

Managing the School Bus Rides

So far, so good. However, Mercy was now beginning to experience difficulties on the bus with some of the students from her own community. Students refused to sit with her or would get up as soon as she sat down in a seat near them. Some of the students threw spitballs at her. When such things occurred, the entire bus of students would erupt in laughter. After the bus driver failed to resolve the situation, she took matters into her own hands. Rather than report these incidents to her principal, she faced the situation head-on. One day, she got out of her bus seat and confronted a student who was throwing spitballs at her. She picked up one of the spitballs and proceeded to stuff it in his face. This caught the attention of the bus driver. It was at this time that he interceded and asked her to return to her seat and then he addressed the incident of throwing of spitballs on his bus. If the bus driver had addressed the situation sooner, this incident would not have escalated to this point. His refusal to acknowledge the situation caused Mercy to become a victim of these attacks and take matters into her own hands.

After the incident was reported to the principal, he instituted a no-nonsense policy that stated that any act of misconduct on the buses or on school grounds would not be tolerated.

As a result of the support Mercy received from the administrators and her teacher, she proceeded to graduate from the eighth grade and went on as an honor student at a high school—back in her community.

ANALYSIS AND TEACHING IMPLICATIONS

Knowing how I felt in the class with all-white males, I know what Mercy endured. For her, these experiences could have felt worse, since she was only a child. She managed to survive in this school only because of her personal efforts and giftedness, but what if she was not courageous enough or gifted?

As a teacher in a similar situation, I would not have tolerated my students snickering or making sarcastic remarks directed at any student regardless of race, ethnicity, or any other factor. First of all, I would have put a stop to that immediately. In the math class, I would have arranged for a graduate student to tutor those students who needed or wanted extra help. In a different setting, I would select groups of students to work together on specific projects or other related activities, making it clear that all students must share responsibilities equally.

Teachers can do many things within the classroom to help minorities feel more comfortable. One of the most important points is for teachers to be innovative in the classroom by incorporating some of the traditions that connect with all students. This could be artwork, books, posters, or other materials that remind students of their culture or heritage. It is also a good idea to have minority guest speakers who can serve as role models to these students.

3

Is There a Minority in the House? Why I Dropped Out of College the First Time Around, *and* Victimized Jones

MARIA C. ABELQUIST

I live in a minority enclave that is predominantly comprised of working-class African American families (85 percent), Latinos (10 percent), and Caucasians (5 percent). My daughter and I are the only Asians in our neighborhood. We purchased a new home in this place that welcomed us with neighborly warmth, southern hospitality, peace, and quiet. I attend a multicultural and nondenominational church located ten minutes away. However, it is within my neighborhood that I visited a church that is attended only by African Americans to have my "minority experience." My aim was to understand what my African American students may experience and feel, and consider what I can do to help my African American students feel comfortable in my classroom.

When Forrest Gump (in the novel and movie) wanted to get "religion" because his shrimp-catching business was floundering, he went to an African American church while living in Louisiana—in the 1960s South. However fictional, I thought that *that* was interesting because whites and blacks did not socialize together in that region and time in American history. But Forrest was on to something. Upon my visit to a Sunday service at Salvation Church, I can understand Forrest's choice because I found the people at the church to be spiritual and soulful.

EXPERIENCING AFRICAN AMERICAN CHURCH SERVICE

The experience I had at the Salvation Church correlated with my perception of African Americans and related to the cultural elements of African Americans in that there was a lot of loud and joyful singing, bodies swaying to the music, ample clapping, folks moving here and there, "comments" made during the sermon (and throughout the service itself) in response to the preacher's words, animated and booming preaching style, long dramatic prayers, and a service that went on for nearly two hours! What an experience! It was like *the* small southern church portrayed in the movie *Forrest Gump*. The preacher and congregation addressed each other as "Sister" and "Brother," and the "Amens!" "Hallelujahs!" and "Yes, Lords!" flew out of people's mouths. From the moment I got out of my car and entered the church, I was in for an experience that I will utilize as a frame of reference in teaching many of my African American students.

I arrived at the church five minutes before the service began at 11 A.M., and I got some curious looks from the church members at the parking lot and into the church building. I felt strange—nothing negative or fearful—being the only non–African American person in the church. There and on that day, I *was* the minority. Although I was accustomed to being around my African American neighbors, I felt strange being in *their* house of worship as if I was intruding in *their* world. I also felt strange because I knew that I was being looked at—however politely—for I could imagine their wonder of my presence—my Asian presence—in the church. I *felt* the eyes on *me*, which led me to feel a bit nervous. And in this new environment with new people, I did what I normally do when I encounter change or something and someone different: I asked questions if I did not know something, and I listened and looked for verbal and visual cues to try to fit in.

In retrospect, I think that I was pretty successful in engaging the members of the congregation. For the most part, the connections were polite greetings, handshakes, hugs, queries, and small talk. I connected with six members of the congregation, including the visiting female pastor (the regular church pastor, who is male, was away on a convention in Atlanta, Georgia). As I entered the church sanctuary, I returned the greeting of one of the ushers (a woman dressed in all-white dress, including white stockings and white gloves—similar to a nurse's outfit). She informed me that there were no church bulletins and gave me a small white envelope for the offering.

Church Sociology

I sat in the middle of one side of the church (there were two columns of pews) and at the center of a long cushioned pew. While getting situated in my seat, I whispered to a woman with a cute bob hairstyle who was sitting in the pew in front of me that I felt underdressed (I came in my usual church garb of shirt, shorts, and flip-flops) as I looked around and saw that nearly *everyone* in the church was dressed in their Sunday finest—formal. The women were wearing dresses, and some even had on fancy hats, while the men were in suits *with* their jackets on in the sweltering July heat! I surely felt inappropriately attired, but the woman to whom I conferred my wardrobe transgression smiled politely and introduced herself and then introduced her uncle who was sitting beside her. She asked for my name and then motioned me to a small sandwich bag full of hard candy that she took out of her purse. "Have some," she said, and I helped myself to one candy. After I finished chatting with her, a woman in a black robe came to my pew and extended her hand, and I shook it. She smiled and stated that her name was Mercy, and she welcomed me to the church. She looked directly in my eyes, gave me a hearty handshake, and sported a wide smile. As it turned out, she was the visiting pastor.

After the service, I caught the attention of a woman dressed in pink. We exchanged greetings and names. She informed me that the keyboardist was her husband. I asked her about her schooling, in reference to the prayer she said aloud in the service. I asked her where she went to school and what she was studying. She replied that she was studying theology and that she was a middle school teacher in a nearby county. Delighted, I told her that *I* was studying to be a middle school teacher, and so we chatted about where we lived and she told me more about herself. We spoke for about five minutes, and our conversation ended with hugs, smiles, and her murmur to "come visit again." After our conversation, I looked around and made eye contact with two women who had been sitting in pews across from mine, and I went up to them and introduced myself. They welcomed me and asked me to come back again.

As I slowly made my way out of the church (after looking around at the end of the service), it was apparent that the members of the congregation were *different* with each other in comparison to how they were with me. They were being polite with me, and I appreciated their warmth. But there was no mistake in the difference as their facial expressions, body language, talk, and laughs transmitted familiarity with each other. They spoke to each other like family and friends, old friends. In fact, I noticed that the congregation was predominantly comprised of senior citizen females. In this small community church (the church had only one Sunday service, with Sunday school preceding the service) that held approximately sixty attendees on the day of my visit, there were fewer than ten females under the age of about thirty (five of them were children and three were teens). Besides, there were fewer than ten males (all except two were under the age of thirty, and the second of the two was a little boy of about eight).

SOME REFLECTIONS

Upon reflection, there were a few surprises I encountered at this traditional African American southern church. First, I was surprised that they had a female preacher even though she was a visiting preacher. I thought that that was interesting and nontraditional. I was also surprised that the people's names were not "Afrikanized" or had an ethnic and racial flair like De'Jon and Shanti. Their names were George, Michael, Sharon, and Sophia—names commonly associated with whites. Here, my hypothesis is that these youth of the civil rights movement were given "white names" by their slave and sharecropper ancestors who also had white names, given to them by their masters. However, it was these "children" of the civil rights era that bestowed the distinct-sounding names to their own children to claim their past and to perhaps give hope to their children in freedom.

MY NONMINORITY EXPERIENCE AS A MINORITY

I think that my visit to the Salvation Church allowed me to feel some semblance of what it is like being the only minority in a situation. I say "semblance" because I did not feel any hostility in reaction to my presence. I felt welcomed (maybe because I am a resident of the neighborhood?) and people were good to me, just like I am treated in my neighborhood. Therefore, the experience I had at the neighborhood church may be atypical because the presence of a minority (especially when one is the only minority) in a situation is not always positive (I have had such encounters in my past and have also observed the awful experiences of others).

Most of the time, I am not aware of my race (and ethnicity) until someone addresses it. In my past experience, attention to my race was usually conveyed in a derogatory and mean-spirited manner when I was a child growing up in Argentina and the United States. While the children slanted their eyes with their fingers and yelled, "Chink!" the adults often began their conversation with me with "You people . . . ." There were very few Asian kids in my elementary, junior high, and high school while I was growing up in New York during the 1970s and early 1980s. A Chinese kid and I were usually the only Asian kids in the entire school (and they were big public schools). Most of my classmates were Caucasian and African American, with a larger number of the former race than the latter. The kids made fun of me and my looks, but I noticed that their negative attention was not always centered on me as they also made fun of each other. The kids had an obsession about calling each other "gay" and poked fun at each other for "being gay." Hence, I somewhat understood that picking on each other was what kids did—and today, I know that all the "players" in the playground are present in the adult world, in workplaces, social circles, and so forth. Therefore, although I observed others who were, I did not feel like I was the "minority" in a situation or a victim until I my first attempt at college in New York.

WHY I DROPPED OUT OF COLLEGE THE FIRST TIME AROUND

As a student at Citizens College, I felt very uncomfortable. In the mid-1980s, a predominant number of Citizens College students were Jewish, and I was an Asian student. There, I felt rejected, shunned, less-than, and avoided by the students because, from my point of view, I did not share their race, religious faith, traditions, and material possessions. My personal impression was that the students I encountered were arrogant, though not proud (there is a difference!), and no one else was good enough for them. I felt that others were considered as not "kosher" and were "infidels." The large number of the Jewish student body was felt everywhere in the school, and I felt that everything in the school catered to Jewish customs and disregarded everyone else. As a student, I felt that the Jewish students did not talk to the non-Jews or Gentiles or acknowledge their minority presence in the school. It felt as if they shunned everyone unlike them. While in attendance, I felt lonely at the school and I felt *less-than* for not being Jewish. I ate alone at the school cafeteria, hardly made any friends (most of the students were commuters), and I eventually dropped out.

My experience with Jewish students should not be taken as an indictment against the entire Jewish community, a group that supported the civil rights movement. I view my personal experience with Jewish students in this college, however, as strange but illuminating, in the context of the minority experience. I thought that as students whose heritage or ethnic group has been perennially discriminated against by anti-Semites and whose people were persecuted in Nazi Germany (and Egypt and during the Inquisition), they would be more empathetic of other minority students. However, I recall that one of the messages of the movie *Planet of the Apes* and George Orwell's book *Animal Farm* was that darkness is part of the human condition, in that the oppressed are capable of becoming the oppressors. As my experience at Citizens College illustrated, that kind of role switching may be carried out by a formerly oppressed group that becomes a predominant or powerful presence. This is the reason why the minority experience is a context-dependent situation.

VICTIMIZED JONES

Indeed, one against many hardly stands a chance, such as in the case of my classmate in junior high school. The memory of my classmate is etched in my mind as a clear example of a situation when a "minority" student exhibited the "minority experience" and "acted the minority."

In junior high school, I had a classmate called Jones. He was an African American with a dark brown complexion, high cheekbones, short dark Afro hair, a broad and wide nose, a thick muscular body, and full thick lips. Jones was jovial—he seemed happy to me at the beginning of each school day—but grew angry as the day progressed, and he spoke with a loud booming voice. Just logistically going to school was a cross-cultural experience to Jones because he was bussed into the predominantly white suburban school—a long bus ride of almost an hour—from his predominantly African American urban neighborhood.

At school, Jones was mercilessly teased, provoked, and bullied by our classmates who were white. I do not remember *any* teachers (who were also white) intervening with the constant bullying Jones experienced. This went on throughout the year (I think it was seventh grade), and Jones got into a lot of fights trying to defend himself against the onslaught of insults that were thrown at him. Kids were calling him horrible things, while walking around like gorillas and making monkey sounds. And, to add insult to injury, Jones was in trouble a lot with the teachers—he was frequently sent to the office. But I do not remember Jones doing anything to incite such treatment from students and teachers. To me, Jones was just Jones. If he had done something wrong or deviant, I would have recalled because the treatment he received was negatively memorable and unrivaled.

While Jones was the only "pure" African American student in my class, it was interesting that we had another classmate, Bob, who was of white and black parentage. No one picked on Bob. In fact, he was one of the popular kids. He was *accepted* by the other kids (white kids) and included in all their activities and conversations. He had a white Jewish mother and a black father, and he looked mostly white. He had light sandy-colored curly hair, very light complexioned skin, was tall, slim, and spoke like a "white" person. He was also soft-spoken, whereas Jones was loud and sometimes did not articulate his words clearly according to the "white" standard. Bob lived in a prestigious neighborhood that was familiar to a lot of Jewish kids (he lived in a predominantly Jewish neighborhood) and always wore nice clothes and looked neat. In contrast, Jones did not wear clothes that were considered stylish in the white school.

Whereas the immediate consequences of the students' and teachers' rejection of Jones was that he was in trouble a lot in school, I also remember that he was a struggling student: I recall that he did not do well in classes. He was expelled once, and I remember not seeing Jones for a while. Looking back, how could he excel in school when he was frequently sent to the office and sometimes expelled? How could he focus on his schoolwork when he had to expend so much energy trying to survive in a predominantly white classroom/school led by white teachers who were hostile to him? He *was* like a fish out of water!

Even as a teenager (and now as an adult), I thought that the way my classmates and teachers treated Jones was horrible, and I can only imagine how Jones felt. I also wonder what happened to him due to the cruelty he was subjected to—I hate to think of it, for the statistics of young black men are dismal.

TEACHING IMPLICATIONS

By all standards of comparison, my experience at my neighborhood church and at Citizens College pale in comparison to what Jones underwent. But if I, as an adult, felt nervous about going into a new situation in which I was the only minority at the Salvation Church and I felt rejected at college due to my Jewish classmates' prejudices, then I can somewhat relate to the feelings that minority students experience in a new environment in which they are the only minority. My recollection of my seventh grade year with Jones and my own experiences help me to understand that minority students (of any race) in my classroom (or school) would feel self-conscious, lonely, afraid, and in need of help and an advocate. In light of my personal experiences and observations of how others were treated in similar situations, I believe that I would be a teacher who is sensitive to classroom and student dynamics, students' diversities, and students' socioeconomic backgrounds, and I would strive to be a bridge to their positive classroom/school experience.

As a teacher, I can help my minority students be more comfortable in my classroom and school by the respectful way I address and speak to my students; the firm, but fair, manner I treat all students; and the benevolent compassion with which I would solve the case-by-case situations my students may embody. I, as a leader, can set a positive and nurturing tone in the classroom by the leadership I establish from the very beginning and throughout the school year. In the classroom, I can set rules and implement a zero-tolerance policy toward bullying. I can also promote a team spirit by mixing the students around in a seating arrangement that sometimes allows them to face each other (so that they can see each other). In the curriculum, I can integrate diverse resources that reflect the diversity represented in the classroom (and in society)—why just read about Western culture? And I can decorate my classroom to reflect that diversity.

As a minority preservice teacher, I would love to see the presence of more minority teachers. If I could, I would also immediately change schools' curriculums so that the content and instruction are not biased toward the preferences of the powerbrokers in society. In addition, I would provide the financial resources teachers need to enrich students' lives and teach without worrying whether they (teachers) can dig any more into their savings to provide materials for classrooms (and provide something other than the prescribed Western literature textbooks!).

POSTSCRIPT

As an end note, I understand that I am sort of an anomaly because I can "fluidly" live in and navigate in other cultures with some ease due to my upbringing, but, by all admissions, situations in which I am the only minority do make me nervous because of the reactions I may sense from the majority. If I had not made a mental note to myself at the Salvation Church (during the service) to make sure to remember the sermon lesson, then I would have forgotten it because I was so focused on my surroundings and in trying to pick up the cues (this is the theory of allocation of cognitive resources, which implies that when people are multitasking on serious tasks, it is difficult to excel in any one of them).

The reception of my presence at the church was positive, but it was not enough to eliminate my feelings. Therefore, this exercise helped me to understand and become determined to be an agent for change for my students in removing barriers to their learning experience. I do not want my students to expend so much mental energy in trying to fit in, or survive (like my classmate Jones), rather than in learning the subject matter (for one of the consequences may be that they opt to drop out, as I did!). Succinctly, I think that understanding the "other" is vital, and I, as a teacher, will seek to understand my students so that I can teach in ways that will help them to reach their highest potential.

4

Seeing My Student at an All-White Church Saved My Day, *and* the Double Lives and Social Consciousness of My White Students

Kalilah Kirkpatrick

As I walked up to the doors of Messiah Lutheran Church, I felt my heart beating faster with each pace. I was walking briskly because I had previously been searching for the entrance from the parking lot and I did not want to be late. I was greeted outside by two elderly white women who still had a slight frown on their face as I reached to open the door. I opened the door to see the sanctuary a few steps away. Everyone was in place (choir, congregation, ushers), the reverend was speaking, and I was the minority.

I attended the 8:00 A.M. service, which was explained on the program as being the "traditional" service. It was filled with a lot of elderly men and women. Their movements were very stiff, and they were alert to the speaker of the hour. The ushers seated me in the third row, which caused the reverend to give me a strange look—a look that I thought communicated that I had interrupted him by entering while he was speaking. As he was speaking, I couldn't help but notice how he was elevated above the congregation in a boxed-in podium. He surveyed the room in a manner that I interpreted as his way of making everyone feel equal and develop a more personal connection with the words. Seated in the third row, I felt several small cramps in my neck, which added to my level of discomfort.

The program was about eight pages long, and they followed it accordingly. The choir sang traditional music, with words and sheet music inside the programs for members and guests to follow along. There were no sounds except from the occasional creek in the wood floor when walked upon.

It's one thing to be the minority, but to feel the minority is a different story. I felt as if all eyes were on me, the environment itself felt strange, and I felt lost. It was out of my comfort zone because I didn't see anyone who looked like me whom I could possibly relate to. I kept my head straight forward in fear that I would not receive a welcoming smile if I established eye contact with anyone. I think my face began to show fear. Suddenly, I felt a hand on my shoulder and a voice said, "Welcome! We are glad to have you!" I politely said, "Thank you," and felt the weight lift off my shoulders.

There were no times during the service that I was able to engage with other members of the church. It almost seemed that one would be kicked out if they disrupted the flow of service. This happened to be Palm Sunday, and communion was being served. As the row behind us got up, they each touched my shoulder as to offer a hand of comfort. I did not participate in communion because I was unsure of the custom. I assumed that they would all drink from the same cup based on a movie I had watched. (It's interesting how media plays a part in our stereotypes, judgments, opinions, preconceived notions, and assumptions.)

After service, one lady who had taken notice of my lack of participation in communion stopped by and commented on it. She said that I didn't have to be afraid to take communion, which made me feel somewhat bad for not doing it. I assured her that I wasn't afraid but would be traveling to my home church to take it. A couple of members came up and shook my hand. Two members suggested that I attend the contemporary services. With that comment, I felt a bit unwanted, thinking that they were trying to place me away from them. On the contrary, maybe they, too, have watched movies or television shows that portray African Americans as having upbeat, oft-screaming church services. I shook the reverend's hand and he said, "You had some great seats! Thanks so much for coming." He made me laugh, and at that moment I felt accepted.

I did notice that certain families had gathered together in a semicircle and seemed to be discussing common topics. As I walked by, their conversation somewhat dwindled, and my feeling of uncertainty in a new environment arose again. There were also some cold faces that made me feel like a visit back to the church would not be a good idea! I related that feeling to bullies in school who intimidate kids who are different from them.

As I walked to my car, I heard someone yell, "Ms. Kirlpatrick!" I turned around, and it was one of my students. Her presence represented the "hero" of the day. What a great feeling to see someone you know!

MY SCHOOLING CONNECTIONS

This experience made me think about my K–12 years of school. I was in a school zone where the majority was Caucasian and the minority was African American. My parents always taught me to be proud of who I am, but I didn't know how to tell them that my classmates weren't judging me by my character, but rather the color of my skin.

Black History Month became the hardest month to bear. The teacher would literally put me on display and pump me for information as if I knew all of the African American history. Inside, I was thinking, "I only know what you teach me," which meant that the limits of my black history knowledge would be confined to Harriet Tubman and Martin Luther King for the next couple of years.

"Feeling" the minority really hit me when I reached middle school. All of my white friends suddenly escaped to their familiar worlds, and that is when I felt segregated and separated. I couldn't figure out how to "fit in" to what was once familiar to me. On the other hand, there was an increase of African Americans in my school. They didn't exactly welcome me with open arms because I had not gone to the same elementary school. I experienced the phenomenon of marginalization—a situation whereby I did not fit in with either the majority or the minority populations.

Discrimination, Deflation of Confidence, and Identity Development

Things were more competitive in middle school. There was this myth that boys were supposed to excel in math and science. Hearing this myth made me that much more focused to outdo the boys. I still remember that day in science class, when we were playing a Jeopardy game to review science terms. I was the representative for my team. I knew my terms and knew that I would come close to winning. The representative of the other team was a boy, and he was pretty smart as well. We were tied, and class was soon to be over. The instructor gave us a tie-breaker question. Whoever raised his or her hand first and answered correctly would win. Sadly, the instructor decided to keep the boys-are-better myth alive! I raised my hand as anxious as I have ever been. He gave the boy another half-second to raise his hand, and he answered the question correctly. My whole team yelled out to the teacher that my hand was first and this was not fair. It didn't matter because my spirit was already defeated. What hurt worse was that my teacher never acknowledged his unfairness and let the other team celebrate with a false victory. Soon after this incident, I began to second-guess myself in classes and never volunteered to be the leader of any group again.

The consequences of feeling gender and racial discrimination took a toll on my confidence. I never felt confident or comfortable in any crowd. I always felt pressure from my black friends and white friends to conform, but I wanted to exist in my own element. I began to view the world as a very unfair place to live in. I became more aware of my surroundings and felt that a multicultural environment was going to harmonize with my personality. During my senior year of high school, I chose to go to a school that was multiracial. I didn't want be pressured into becoming a part of a particular social group based on my race alone. I was seeking freedom to be who I wanted to be and hang out with whom I wanted to. I developed relationships with people from all types of backgrounds that I could learn from. I found friendships that would allow us to talk comfortably without operating from assumptions. We were able to ask each other questions that would break down the thick walls of stereotyping that society had imposed on us. Some people don't ever feel comfortable being the minority, but experiencing the minority in my early years of school shaped my determination to be satisfied with myself and do things to the best of my ability.

THE DOUBLE LIVES AND SOCIAL CONSCIOUSNESS OF MY WHITE STUDENTS

I teach at a school where the minority races comprise the majority. Many of my students have exhibited the "minority experience." The first thing that I notice is the assimilation. The minority (white) students tend to take on the characteristics of the majority so they don't feel like outcasts. Some of these students seem to have a double life. I actually asked a student one day why he feels like he needs to act like everyone else. He responded that not taking part would cause too many problems for him socially. I have a lot of Hispanics in my classroom who often *code-switch*: They love their culture and always stay true to their native language when with their Hispanic friends. However, they also know it's important for a teacher to understand them so they can receive the appropriate grade.

I started teaching more current events this year, and of course, there are several racial issues that emerge when discussing the power of the media. One of my students raised his hand and said, "Why do they always show black people as committing all of the crimes? I can tell you about five white people who should be on the headlines." At this point, I knew that my students really were hurt by seeing minorities in the news constantly. I knew they were not colorblind anymore and realized the hurt and the mistreatment that came with being the minority. They felt that they would always be viewed as criminals because media reports were centered on minorities and crimes. Being a minority myself, my students look to me for all the answers, and because they do, I make it a point to be friendly to all the teachers at school so as to be able to know their issues. I show my students kindness and fairness, but I demand respect—which they return in kind. I want to show them that they don't have to place themselves in a box, but rather step outside and see that the world is not a square but a circle. What I leave with them every day is that they should always believe in themselves and make good decisions, and the outcome will be great.

FINAL REFLECTIONS

After reflecting on my minority experiences, I understood how my students feel. I really felt that I owed them an apology for not taking time to understand the emotional roller coaster they undergo as the minority students. I especially thought about my English learners who struggle with the complexities of the English language. I was hard on them because I expected them to know certain things, but they did not. Even now, I still get frustrated when trying to teach them because I see them communicating actively in the hallways, but when they step into my class, they become inactive and do not participate in class work. That's how I felt in that third pew in that church, that day. I felt as if there was such a great expectation for me to know when to pull the prayer bench out, that communion was mandatory and not voluntary, that not being in place before the reverend begins to talk was disrespectful. All those were things I didn't know but was "expected" to know. I thought about my black students who struggle every day with their place in society—feeling like they can't be "too black" and they can't "act white." That's how I felt on that pew that morning. I felt like apologizing to all my students if I made them feel more awkward than normal because they, too, were having a racial identity crisis. I saw my lesson plans changing to incorporate more resources that honor *all* my students. I wanted to change so that they would feel welcomed in the doors of my classroom and enable them to open up their windows of opportunity.

Sitting in that third row has changed my perspective about teaching. I should be more diligent in creating a classroom setting that doesn't intimidate my students. If I see minority students who need to connect with other students, I will encourage them to do so because that will help them to feel more comfortable and will increase their participation and academic performance. Outside the classroom, I can have general conversations in which I can ask them about their home culture and traditions. This will give me personal connections with them and will make them feel like they are important and not lost in the crowd. Without them asking, I could spend a little more time at their desks talking them through their assignments. Oftentimes, I think of my students as independent people, but they still are children who relish attention.

If I could change one thing right now, I would change society's view of race to being beautiful, as opposed to being controversial. This would allow people to feel comfortable in their own skins without feeling the need to go through a metamorphosis to fit them. It would also empower us as a whole to achieve every dream we've dreamed, goal we are trying to reach, and mountains we wish to climb. I wish *minority* and *majority* were terms that were not in the dictionary because they create too much division. If the world won't give my students equality, then it is my duty to provide them that in my classroom, by all means necessary.

5

Experiencing the White Church, A Cross-Cultural Wedding Experience, *and* A New Angela: A Bicultural Personality

AJA' PHARR

I did not know what to expect as I walked into Cross Presbyterian Church, a white congregation. I had already imagined that it would not be anything like St. Moses Baptist Church, where I worship each Sunday. St. Moses is an all-black church that presents the traditional black church experience. The first word that comes to mind when comparing these two churches would be *different*. Cross Presbyterian Church has two services; one is traditional and the other is contemporary. Recently, I decided to visit the traditional service.

The traditional service followed an agenda very closely. The congregation sang songs softly from a hymnal. There was no choir during this service; the congregation simply sang to provide the music. After the singing, the pastor read from the Scriptures and then read his sermon from the pulpit. She remained behind the pulpit and occasionally looked up from her notes. Once the service was over, some members of the congregation talked very quietly to each other, but most of them filed out of the church. There was not much excitement. Rather, the environment felt more like a business-professional meeting. The pastor stood at the front door and shook hands as the congregants departed the building.

A Reflective Comparison

Being the minority in the room felt a little weird, no matter how much I tried to fight it. First of all, I felt overdressed. I wore a black suit with pantyhose and pumps. I carried my clutch on one side and my Bible case on the other. I had spent extra time putting on makeup and styling my hair to perfection. At Cross Presbyterian Church, however, the members were wearing jeans, khakis, sundresses, capris, sandals, and even sneakers. As I approached the church, two older white men ran up to shake my hand. They probably knew that I was a stranger who was out of my element. I wanted to run to my car and call it a day, but I was determined to walk slowly enough to take this all in.

I went inside the church building. Although no one else spoke, I felt like a million eyes were on me. I began thinking, "Why did I get curls in my hair this time? Why did I wear these dressy pumps? Why did I not sit closer to the door so that I would not have to walk so far to get out of here? Should I have waited for the contemporary service? Did I hear someone say 'black'?" I knew that I was imagining things.

I was not successful in communicating with members of the congregation. Most of the people who participated in this service were older, white, middle-class people. I believe that I was the only new face among people who knew everything there was to know about each other. I could tell that it was not normal for a black person to visit this church.

I must admit that the church members seemed like very nice people. I wonder if I was acting in such a way that I appeared to be unapproachable. I was so used to hugs and kisses from my church members. Visitors do not get out of my church without at least a few hugs from the members of the church. We actually hug each other during church as a part of the order of service. The pastor will take a few moments to instruct the congregation to turn around to the people in front, beside, and behind them and give them a hug. Even if you decide not to stand and walk around, someone will run up to you, hug you, and say, "God bless you," or "Good morning." I noticed some people at Cross Presbyterian Church talking closely, being sure not to get too loud, but I only saw two people hugging. If anything at all, there was a lot of handshaking. I do not think that the way I was being treated had anything to do with me being black; it appears that the members of this congregation felt more comfortable talking to people they knew.

Some Surprises

Although there were obvious differences, I did not witness anything too surprising while at this church. However, when the service went from point A to point B without any interruptions, I found that to be somewhat surprising. In my church, after the choir sings, there might be a word from the pastor that will reflect on the message of the song, or someone might say "Amen" or even cry out to God in praises of thanksgiving. The musicians, on their own inspiration, might add to the praises by beating harder on the drums or changing the tune of the music as the worshippers dance in celebration of the goodness of the Lord. The service will actually take another direction from that of the program as the "Holy Spirit" begins to direct the service. Because there were no interruptions of this sort and we seemed to be on a strict schedule, I walked into this service at 8:45 A.M., and the service was over within one hour! That is unheard of at my church or any black church I have ever visited—not even for midweek services.

The second notable surprise was that the congregants only responded out loud when they were reading a script. The leader would read something from the program, and the congregants would respond in unison only when it was their turn to speak. This was the only time I heard the church say "Amen." The "Amen" was also scripted at the end of the reading. Compared to my church, where you could hear voices at any time—voices crying out and people stomping their feet and clapping their hands without any permission at all—I was surprised at how noisy and chaotic my church seemed to be compared to this church. I felt uncomfortable when I had to sneeze a few times due to my allergies. I thought that everyone was offended by my sneeze, which actually snuck out "without permission" because I definitely tried to hold it in for a while. No one said "God bless you" because I don't think it is appropriate to say much of anything at this church.

The last thing I noticed was that there was not much movement at all. At my church, worshippers wave their hands, choirs rock from side to side, and the preacher walks up and down the aisles during his message. We walk around to hug each other, pay our tithes and offering, and visit the altar during the service. At Cross Church, I only stood during two hymns. I guess this was fine, though, because the service was short and to-the-point. I never had a chance to feel wiggly or restless.

Some Reflections for the Classroom

Once I got into my car, I thought about how this experience related to my classroom. Maybe this explained why my white students in my predominantly white classes were so calm and did not need much entertainment. Maybe this had something to do with them being able to stay in their seats and listen to a lecture. On the other hand, was this why my black students had to always be making beats on the desk or seemed to feel the need to get up whenever they wanted to? Did this explain why they needed shorter lectures but would rather have group work? Had I found the answer to why my black students were so affectionate and wanted hugs, while my white students never reached out for me?

A CROSS-CULTURAL WEDDING EXPERIENCE

Another time that I felt that I was the minority in a situation was when I attended the wedding of a white friend of mine. We attended high school together, and although I was not very close to her, I was invited to her wedding through another person: a very close white friend.

I was extremely excited to be invited to this wedding and had expressed to my mother that I would tell her all the details. I had witnessed many weddings on television, but I had only been to a black wedding. This wedding was taking place at a historical church. Although she was not a member here, she had rented out this very old church for her special day. I walked into the church with my close friend's mother and sat with her during the service. Once again, I felt overdressed. I thought I looked gorgeous, but I was not in the wedding! Most people were dressed nicely, but they could have easily visited a casual restaurant later. I, however, was dressed for a royalty visit. I looked around as the service began, and, just as I had predicted, I was the only black person! I felt fine, though. I knew I looked good and I held my head high.

Extra Careful for Appearances' Sake

Once the short ceremony was over, I did not feel as comfortable in the reception as I did in the church. I do not know if it was because everyone was mingling and I was not, or if it was because I stood out. I grabbed a glass of wine and sat at a table. I was careful not to talk with my mouth full and to wipe my mouth as often as possible. I smiled occasionally when people walked by our table and spoke very slowly and carefully as to enunciate my words to perfection. I was very aware of my actions and left to use the restroom twice to check on my face.

With all the mental energy drained from me at the wedding, I was a little tense when I left the event. I kicked off my shoes as soon as I got into my car. I also stopped to get something to eat because I had eaten like a bird at the reception. There was plenty of food, but it did not think it was appropriate to pile my plate up. I called my mom after everything was over and told her about the entire wedding day. The first thing that I expressed to her was that I think I would have liked it more had I taken her with me.

THE LONE BLACK STUDENT IN AN ADVANCED CLASS

One situation that comes to mind when I recall a student "experiencing the minority" was when I first started teaching three years ago. My honors classes were predominantly white, with only a handful of black students, and Angela was one of them. Like me, this was her first year at Richtown High School. Angela was extremely articulate and very smart. She was a loner because she appeared to prefer working alone to group work. I could always depend on Angela to do her work with perfection. When she entered the room or spoke aloud, her black counterparts would always snicker, but the white students seemed to accept her for who she was. She dressed very casually, wore her hair very straight, and could even be seen with a flower at times. Her look more closely resembled that of my white students, rather than my black students.

One day, while teaching about personal narratives, Angela volunteered to share her story. Among other things, she spoke about the relationship she left behind when she moved to North Carolina. She had dated a white guy, and she felt that her parents disapproved of that relationship. She added that they were hoping that she would find someone of the same race. After the students heard this part of her story, they really treated her differently. While the white students took her into their circle, the black students treated her like a complete outcast. To them, she was "acting white." They commented that she "talked white," "dressed white," and now she did not even like the guys of her own race.

For some time, Angela did not seem to care about these social issues. She continued to have her own style and spoke Standard English. She continued to score high on exams and projects, and I recommended her for many awards. During the second year, I did not have Angela in my class; however, I saw her in the halls and I was friends with her counselor.

A New Angela: A Bicultural Personality

After the summer, Angela returned to high school with a different attitude. Where had it come from? She had a new group of black friends, joined a step group that was made up of black students only, and had started dating a popular black guy. I also noticed that Angela was wearing what was considered black hairstyles and black clothing styles. In my opinion, she was not being herself at all. I knew it would be a matter of time before this changed. Angela seemed happy, though, and grew very popular within the school's black community.

This year—her senior year—I watched her as she gained more and more confidence. She was still very brilliant and determined not to hide it. She was in the run for valedictorian and had joined many diverse clubs. She, once again, had her own style. All of the students knew her because of her intelligence. She began to date another white guy and has been very happy. She has learned to be herself no matter what. She has learned not to conform to society's belief of how you should talk, dress, or act as a minority.

During graduation, she will cross the stage near the top of her senior class, and students from all backgrounds will be cheering for her. I don't think many students will be focused on the terms *traitor* or *fake*, as she gets her diploma. I think there will be more talk of her attending a university on a full scholarship and how she is so wonderful for just being herself—Angela.

ANALYSIS FOR TEACHING DIVERSE LEARNERS

In the forthcoming book *Teaching Diverse Learners* by Charles Hutchison, it is noted that "by high school, students would have developed both the intellectual and physical capacity to enter the immersion-emersion stage" of Cross's identity development, a stage characterized by the exclusion of other races and the wearing of identifiably ethnic clothing (p. 117). I have worked at Richtown High School for the past three years. Richtown is a majority white school, unlike the predominantly black high school where I graduated from in 1997. I often feel sorry for the black students at Richtown because I feel that they are not receiving the wonderful high school experience that I did when I was in school. The black students at Richtown feel as if they are just there. Most of them hate that school and openly express it. They show no signs of school pride and just try to get by. They have many discipline problems and failing grades. Even the black students who are not in my classes try to get to know me and frequently visit my classroom. They often beg to stay in my classroom all day, but I cannot allow them to do that.

The black students claim that their other teachers are racist and do not care about them. In response to that, I help them to understand that not every teacher is willing to give the "tender care" that I give them. I let them know that they cannot expect to be treated as "special" by every teacher because the real world does not operate that way. I ask them to become self-motivated and strive to make the grade. Many of these students want to know that they are loved and cared about before they perform in the classroom.

Many of the black students easily get bored with the curriculum of an all-white school. Most of the teachers at Richtown High School are white. In the English department, novels are chosen by the teachers. As long as these novels are at or near grade level, they are acceptable. Having taken a children's literature course in college, I know the importance of using multicultural literature in my classroom. I want to be sure to reach all students. I have used Sandra Cisneros's *House on Mango Street*, Adeline Mah's *Chinese Cinderella*, Walter Dean Myers's *Monster*, and Virginia Hamilton's *Brother Rush*. I am careful not to choose my books over the summer, but rather wait until I meet my students first. I want to know what my classes look like before choosing what we will read. Of course, we have to read Shakespeare's *Romeo and Juliet* because it is a major ninth grade work. However, the way I approach it will depend on what my classes look like.

I want my classes to be interesting for all students and for all my students to be able to relate to something in the course. It is important to me that students feel valuable by being able to contribute something to the course and getting something out of it. It made me really feel special, yet sad at the same time, when a black male who was repeating eleventh grade gave me his thoughts after reading the book *Monster* in class. He said, "Ms. Pharr, this is the first novel I have ever read all the way through."

Moving Students from Silence to Success

I think my minority students feel comfortable in my classroom because I strive to make it a comfortable and safe environment. There was one student, Mario, who was seventeen years old but in my ninth grade English class. Not only was he much older, but he looked much older as well. Students often asked him his age and why he was in *their* class. He stayed to himself and remained very quiet at first. After I made it clear to my students that we would not talk about each other and would have respect for every person, Mario began to participate and excel in the class.

Tunde, a West African migrant student, was also very quiet in class in the beginning of the school year. She never wanted to read aloud, and when she did, she often spoke in a whisper. I eventually learned that she did not want the other students to hear her accent. It only took one time for students to laugh, and I handled that issue immediately. From that point on, Tunde gained confidence and was an excellent performer in class.

In my classroom, I think that I can help minority students feel more comfortable by opening up the floor for more discussion. I realize that Room 910 is not my classroom; it is their classroom! I do not like giving my opinion for very long. I would rather hear the opinion of my students. I enjoy using the fishbowl strategy or Socratic seminar in my classes. I like to hear the students make comments and give their ideas. Students need to feel like they are making the lesson their own. Classes are made up of people from many backgrounds and personalities. We can all learn from each other, and this is so much better than getting the opinion of only the instructor.

I think that I can help minority students more by encouraging their participation in extracurricular activities and clubs. Students should not limit themselves to the classroom setting but should be willing to interact with other groups. Many of my black students at Richtown refuse to participate in any activities besides basketball, football, and NAACP Club. When I return to school in the evenings to see a production by the Drama Club, I do not see any diversity on stage. When I attend a Poetry Club meeting, there are only whites there. However, it is the absolute reverse at the NAACP functions, which are only attended by blacks. I want to encourage the ninth graders to enter Richtown with an open mind. I want them to realize that Richtown was built for *all* students and that they do not have to act as the minority even if they are the minority.

ADVICE FOR ADMINISTRATORS

Right now, if I could change something, I would hire more black teachers at Richtown. The freshman year is the toughest year for many students, and incidentally, most of the repeaters are black students. I really believe that it would benefit students if they could have teachers who share their cultural values and look and think like them.

Professional education schools can offer prospective teachers as many classes as they want to on diversity in the classrooms, but until teachers and administrators are willing to get to know their students individually and bypass the color of their skin, things are going to remain the same. Based on my observations, when students feel mistreated or unequal in the classroom, they tend to have lower grades. I often think of how my black students feel in my honors classes and agree with many educators who believe that our children are worth whatever it takes to make them successful!

6

A Black Female in a Predominantly White Male Class, *and* Reversing Roles: A White Student Acting the Minority in Class

LISA MCCRIMMON

Being a black woman who is a member of an African Methodist Episcopal Zion Church, I had the experience of attending a white church not far from my home. Festival Church is an evangelical community church, unaffiliated with a denomination. My experience on this Sunday morning was both similar to and different from what I've experienced at my own church.

THE WHITE CHURCH EXPERIENCE

The predominantly white congregation at Festival Church was very comfortable with each other. As an aspiring math teacher, I felt it important prior to the service to count the number of people in attendance. I counted about eighty-five people, of whom four were African American, including myself. I enjoyed the service very much. Even though there was a difference in the worship style I am used to, the experience of worshipping the same God is universal. I acknowledge, however, that there may be several cultural factors that encourage normative behavior within any group of people.

While at Festival Church, I made mental notes of some cultural elements and the way they manifested in behavior. There was limited talking in this church. At one point, the pastor asked the congregation a question and encouraged them to discuss it quietly among their neighbors for few minutes. He then asked for volunteers to share with the group what issues were brought up in their private discussions. Finally, he tied several of the responses he received to the theme of the sermon. This experience was different, because I am more familiar with Sunday service being reserved for the pastor to speak. I am accustomed to a congregation that worships by clapping, singing, and other forms of praise, where discussion is limited and reserved for Bible study on Wednesday nights. In direct opposition to this encouragement of discussion, I recall one pastor making a comment about "popcorn-people," which is a term reserved for those who felt the need to pop up out of their seats to speak. I found this service to embrace teaching as well as worship.

Anxiety Defused by Jan's Welcome

Prior to the start of the service, a woman approached me. She introduced herself as Jan, and welcomed me. My first emotion was relief. I had concern about attending a church alone, where I was sure to be a minority, which is why I probably delayed it until the very last possible moment. Apparently, there is comfort in being surrounded by peers with whom one has something in common. I had built up a certain level of anxiety while walking across the parking lot and entering the doors. Jan managed to defuse some of that anxiety by acknowledging me.

Singing is a big part of most worship services. My home church belongs to a denomination where massive choirs are the norm. Festival Church had four members who sang at the start of service, aided by microphones and instrumental music that was amplified. I enjoyed the music, although it was different from what I am accustomed to. This music was more contemporary, and the congregation was welcomed to sing along, with the lyrics projected onto a large screen. I was impressed with the use of technology in worship service at such a small church. I had seen the use of technology at other churches before, even minority churches, but the congregational size of the churches was always quite large. In fact, before attending Festival Church, I researched a little about it on the Internet, and I was quite impressed with its website. The caliber of the website caused me to believe that the church was larger than it actually was. In keeping with the church's use of technology, at the beginning of the service, a PowerPoint presentation was used to honor the male members, since this was Father's Day. It showed them helping in the community and on missionary projects.

Preaching According to Culture?

The preaching style is an area that I would classify as being the most notable in defining the cultural makeup of the congregation. Had I been blindfolded and unable to detect if the pastor was black or white by the sound of his voice, the preaching style would have quickly identified the congregation as white. As noted previously, the preaching was more of a teaching, and not necessarily a measure to draw the congregation into worship by means of escalated voices, clapping, stomping, and dancing. In many traditional "black" churches—and increasingly in some charismatic white churches—these activities are included in what is called "shouting" and are viewed as a part of the highest forms of praise and worship.

Being the minority in the room, I felt self-conscious. I was keenly aware that I was different, and I made a conscious effort not to emphasize my dissimilarities by behaving any differently from those around me. This turned out to be a fairly simple task, since those around me were not behaving any differently than I would if I was at my own church.

Reconnecting with Jan and Others

At the close of service, Jan reapproached me to finish our earlier conversation. This made me feel as though our initial encounter was genuine and not a ploy to find out who the "new black lady" was. Although I'm sure she was intrigued at seeing me, she showed that she was really interested in getting to know me and making me feel welcomed. Accompanied by her kind words, her actions demonstrated this as well. She allowed the conversation to venture off into telling me quite a bit about herself and her family.

On my way to the parking lot, I was approached by another woman who introduced herself as Tish and walked with me through the parking lot in order to spend time with me. She invited me to her house the next Sunday evening for dessert and coffee. She explained that during the summer, many of the ministries took a break and the next formal "Women's Ministry" meeting wouldn't be until September. Since several visitors had attended church, she decided to have a forum where the women could stay in touch.

Overall, the members of the church seemed very connected. They were not as cordial to me as with each other, but I still felt welcomed. Initially, I felt overwhelmed by the encounters with Jan and Tish. However, upon further discussion with Tish, I discovered that Jan was a leader in the Women's Ministry, and Tish was the pastor's wife. These two women in prominent positions made me feel welcomed. As opposed to looking at our conversations as must-do tasks, I chose to accept their kindness as acts of friendship and love. Surprising, the other three African Americans, who were all female as well, did not make any attempt at any form of communication with me.

BLACK FEMALE IN A PREDOMINANTLY WHITE MALE CLASS

As an undergraduate in college, I once found myself as the minority in a political science course entitled "Civil Rights and Liberties." Most of the students taking this class were aspiring lawyers, and were mostly young white males. The professor was also a white male. As if the required readings weren't hard enough (legalese and all), the class participation and discussions were other areas of anxiety. Imagine reading a case about civil liberties in education or the rightfulness of affirmative action as an African American woman, and basing your argument on the cultural experiences you've encountered in your life to a class full of white males. Needless to say, I avoided commenting or discussing my briefs (which we were instructed to write after each case reading), at all costs. The professor, being sensitive to my presence, purposefully made sure that my viewpoints were introduced, discussed, and sometimes even argued whenever appropriate.

Clumsy Misrepresentation of Self

My first recollection of this experience is how I used to fumble around with my vocabulary, in an attempt to make sure that the words I spoke were acceptable and understood by my classmates. I tried to hide my emotions when discussing anything so that I wouldn't be judged or, worse yet, appear to be stereotypical. Thinking back, this behavior must have made me appear nonchalant or uncaring, when indeed most of the topics in discussion were things that piqued my inner interest and beliefs. At the pretense of not exaggerating my differences, I may have clumsily *misrepresented* my true feelings.

Suspecting that I would behave in such a manner as the minority in class, or perhaps recognizing it for what it truly was (a downplay of my true feelings), the professor would cleverly argue my viewpoint from an anonymous point of view, paving the way for me to comfortably state my assertions. I ended up thoroughly enjoying this class. I think my classmates learned a lot, probably more so from me that I did from them, as their experiences were already outlined throughout the text.

One day after one class, a white female approached me and said that she didn't understand a lot of the cases until she had opportunity to hear my interpretation in class. I still don't know if my interpretation facilitated her understanding because I am female or because I'm black. Maybe both realities led to her understanding.

Consequent to these dynamics, I ended up getting an A in a rather difficult class. I believe, in part, that it was because I was placed in a position to offer a different viewpoint than what was "norm" in classroom discussions, thanks to a good instructor.

REVERSING ROLES: A WHITE STUDENT ACTING THE MINORITY IN CLASS

In a class I was observing, there was an inclusion student in a "low-achieving" mathematics class. He was a white child in a class of minority students (both Hispanic and black). Jeremy was, in this case, the minority. He acted out by talking out of turn, disrupting the class every chance he got. At one point, he even went to sleep. When the teacher attempted to wake him, he declared, "This class is boring!" Needless to say, the teacher became extremely frustrated. She asked that he quietly work on a homework assignment. He took this as permission to go back to sleep. I could see the frustration building within the teacher because Jeremy's behavior was enticing the other students to tune her out and do their own thing as well. I remember feeling sorry for the teacher and wondering why a separate class wasn't designed for students such as this young man.

After watching this drama unfold for several minutes, I volunteered to help Jeremy complete his homework assignment in the back of the room. He was reluctant at first. However, after the teacher informed him of his options (either accept my offer, or go the office) he opted for help from me.

I was amazed at how bright Jeremy was. His issue seemed to be less of an inability to do the work than it was being starved for attention. After modeling the first problem for him, he seemed desperate to want to prove to me that he could do the rest of the problems without any help. Whenever he got stuck, I saw what one would describe as fear on his face. When I attempted to help by talking him through it, he seemed to suddenly get an "I know that already" attitude. I didn't make a big deal about his on-again, off-again behavior, although it was rather difficult to stifle my own "I told you so" attitude. Fortunately, the remaining forty-five minutes of class were rather peaceful and quite productive.

Coping with the Minority Experience with Behavioral Emotional Dysfunction

On consequent visits to this classroom during my clinical observation, I tutored Jeremy in the back of the classroom with either homework or incomplete class assignments and got to know him quite well. My experience with him taught me about the importance of a teacher's individual attention to a student. I have wondered about what happens to other students in similar situations who do not have the availability of a student teacher or observer who can help tone down the behavioral issues.

I believe that Jeremy had anxieties being the only white student in a class full of minority students. This reverse cultural experience in the classroom not only had him thrown into an environment to which he was not accustomed (sole white student in a class full of minorities), but academically, he was also thrown into a classroom with students who were classified as underachievers, although in a healthier frame of mind, he was capable of performing better. I think Jeremy acted out as a coping mechanism to survive his current situation, without the coping skills required to endure it.

CONCLUDING THOUGHTS

Thinking about the experience I had while at Festival Church, I recognize that even though I may have experienced similar emotions that minority students experience in the classroom, I still had an advantage: I was an adult. My experience was also a one-time event. However, minority students endure participation in classes on a daily basis, year after year. Student success in class—which is partly determined by their emotional states—is the foundation of their grade, which in turn affects their advancement, higher education, and potential life outcomes. Therefore, it is vital for teachers to help students to be comfortable, sometimes by just acknowledging their presence. This can go a long way in letting their guards down. The kindness extended to me at Festival Church made me feel welcomed and helped me to focus on the similarities rather than the differences between myself and the members. I plan to offer the same kindness and acceptance to all the students in my class.

7

Self-Conscious at Pleasant Greens, *and* Minding Mandy, the White Minority in Class

CARLETTA BRADLEY

Pleasant Greens Baptist Church members have frequently placed invitations throughout my community in reference to special services. This paper provided me an opportunity to visit. Based on the cars I saw in the parking lot and the well-kept church graveyard filled with large granite headstones from decades past, I gathered the predominant church culture to be white.

In my personal interactions with white people, I have found them to be mostly conservative in manner, speech, and dress. I have also found them to have strong adherence to administrative and organizational plans of action. Therefore, before walking through the doors of Pleasant Greens Baptist Church (PGBC), I supposed I would witness a flawless service of no more than one-and-one-half hours where the musical selections would be well rehearsed with no room for "spiritual sprees" and a conservatively dressed congregation sitting quietly through a three-point sermon that would be read, well prepared, and succinct.

Upon entering the church, I found many of my assumptions to be true. The entire congregation was nicely dressed. No one wore jeans or T-shirts. Even the male children wore dress shirts and khaki shorts, while the girls wore summer dresses or blouses with skirts. There were no loud splashes of color. I expected to see a choir. However, I speculated on the difficulty of having choir members commit during summer months, especially in smaller churches. Interestingly enough, there was a worship team that consisted of three singers, a pianist, a drummer, and a brass ensemble. Musical transitions were seamless and on cue, as the main worship leader (the pianist) flipped from page to page in his binder of written sheet music.

As I imagined, the sermon contained three main points; however, instead of reading it in its entirety, the pastor only read scriptures and lengthy stories. The sole interjections from the congregation were laughter in response to the pastor's jokes.

Self-Conscious at Pleasant Greens

The congregation seemed to be genuinely welcoming and friendly. Before I was seated, my hand was firmly shaken by five ushers or "greeters." I quickly found a seat near the rear and slid halfway down the row, leaving room for others. Those sitting in front of me and on the same pew all welcomed me warmly, as did those who slid in next to me just before the service officially began.

When the pastor asked first-time visitors to raise their hand to receive a welcome package, I did not respond. After returning home, I reflected on why I had not raised my hand. After all, I first visited my present church about one-and-a-half years ago and remember raising my hand when offered a visitor package. As I reasoned, I determined that I was not ashamed; I am who I am and I'm quite pleased with that. I wasn't afraid; the congregants didn't display hostility or discontent toward me. I didn't misunderstand the directions; they were clearly and simply given. After reading chapter 3 of Hutchison's *Teaching Diverse Learners*, I became aware that I was not like the majority of worshippers present. Therefore, my cognitive capacity became overtaxed, and so I could not think quickly enough to determine an appropriate action for my given situation. In other words, I was thinking about a course of action while self-conscious. Before I knew it, the ushers distributing packets for first-time visitors had passed my row. I thought if I raised my hand at this point, I would appear foolish, so I sat quietly, as did the rest of the congregation. Although the ushers knew I had never been there before, a package was not forced on me. For that, I was grateful.

Concerned about Self-Presentation

Knowing that I would be walking into a foreign church environment that Sunday morning, my behaviors and mind-set became altered when my clock alarm signaled it was time to get ready for church. This altered mind-set (anxiety) later affected my actions during the service.

I attend a large, six-year-old nontraditional church that has people from various races not only in the congregation but also ministering from the stage and in church leadership positions. Some people come to church in jeans and T-shirts, while others wear dress suits with hats and feathers, so I can dress up either nicely or casually and know that I will fit in.

My assumptions regarding the members of PGBC robbed a portion of my free choice this particular Sunday morning. Knowing what stereotypes exist regarding black people, I had just one chance for a first impression to represent myself well. I needed to dress in a manner that would attract the least amount of attention, assimilate into the congregants, and portray myself as an educated and respectable black woman. I had to take on an active role of acting who I really was in order to deflect possible negative connotations. Furthermore, knowing that there is an expectation of blacks operating on CPT (colored people's time), I had to make sure that I was early for the service.

Action and Reaction?

There was a mutual discomfort as the members of the congregation came around to shake my hand during the "greeting." While they hugged, embraced, laughed, and joked with each other, they only extended their hand to me and said the same thing, "Hello" or "Welcome." No one asked my name, if I was visiting from out of town, what brought me to the church, or anything else.

I must confess that I did not do any more than return the handshake and respond with "Hello" or "Thank You." Although I knew it was customary and appropriate to say more, *I couldn't think fast enough* to know what was appropriate for me to say to them. Therefore, I was not able to engage or connect with any of them beyond the level of superficial congeniality.

MINDING MANDY, THE WHITE MINORITY IN CLASS

Last year, I taught two sessions of mixed choir, each of which lasted for one semester. Mandy was one of the students who took the class both semesters. During the first semester, Mandy was always very quite and reserved. She appeared well mannered, even tempered, and a diligent worker. I knew that Mandy was from a low-income white family, so I purchased her some pants and skirts from Goodwill and found formal wear for her to wear at our concerts. Additionally, I provided complimentary tickets to her mother and sisters. After our performances, her mother would always find me to tell me how much she appreciated what I had done to help Mandy.

During second semester, Mandy came into class as the only seasoned chorister. Additionally, her younger sister Susan was in the class. Mandy and Susan were very chatty, which led to me separating the two of them. Besides, the new choral students were all freshmen and mild-mannered, so Mandy was able to lord over them. Her grades dropped significantly, and she had to be sent to the office or out in the hall on various occasions. The mother who once sang my praises stormed into the school office demanding an explanation for my ill treatment of her child. After a more civilized conversation with the mother, I learned that Mandy had had significant problems throughout her school history with bullying and fighting.

In retrospect, I realized that during the first semester, Mandy found herself as an underclassman and a minority. In her class were the well-loved black girls, the middle-class honors dance and theater students who were white, and the boys. Mandy, the overweight, low-income white freshman girl, was tolerated by the others but never fully embraced. She therefore kept to herself, did her work, and excelled academically. Nevertheless, if I had known some of the things I know now about diverse learners, I would have worked harder to break up the cliques in my class and helped to build Mandy's self-confidence. One important lesson Mandy's example taught me is that students experiencing the minority effect may go undetected as they excel academically, even as they are failing in far worse ways.

TEACHING IMPLICATIONS OF MY CHURCH AND MANDY'S EXPERIENCES

Addressing Mental Stumping

My brief encounter with mental "double-pedaling" or "mental stumping" when asked to be identified as a first-time visitor has made me sensitive to the fact that I may ask a simple direct question to a minority learner and receive a blank stare or no response at all. Their hesitancy may not necessarily imply that they do not know the answer or that they did not hear the question. Rather, they may be processing how to respond appropriately. Instead of pressing this student for an immediate answer, I might tell the student we will come back to him or her and ask other students to respond. I also might ask the student to write his or her response down on a sheet of paper and then walk over to view what the student has written. This approach would lower the student's stakes if he or she was wrong and offer "think time." Furthermore, I could provide additional questions to help the student narrow the list of possible appropriate responses, thereby guiding his or her thinking.

All in My Head

Despite the fact that the congregants of PGBC responded warmly toward me, I still knew I was a minority in the room and felt out of place, as if all eyes were on me. I don't think there is anything that the churchgoers could have done differently in the ninety minutes we spent together that could have caused me to embrace them more or to feel truly embraced. However, I felt comfortable and welcome enough that I have thought about going back to the church on a Sunday night, when I am not in my regular church. With that said, I believe that a "safe" classroom cannot be contrived in a single session but that time and consistent bridging is necessary.

I did not begin thinking about the church service as I walked in the doors of PGBC; I began mentally preparing myself to enter the minority experience as I got ready for church, drove down the road, parked my car, walked to the front door. I had the opportunity to prepare myself mentally as well as physically; I had a choice of clothing to wear in order to better assimilate. As a teacher of low-income students, I am more sensitive to the fact that they do not have time to mentally prepare to enter the class. A majority of their energies are devoted to surviving another day. Also, they may not have the financial resources to be dressed in the latest fashion. Therefore, when they arrive in my classroom, they may be doing what I had at least two hours to do before entering a potentially "hostile" environment.

Misbehavior as a Coping Mechanism

Mandy, my minority student, felt isolated, and therefore chose to separate herself as her coping mechanism during her first semester with me. I was not effective in reaching her because I did not realize that she was only playing a role to fit into the classroom culture. I believe that during my first semester with Mandy, if I were more successful in raising her self-esteem (both in her own eyes and before her peers), she would not have taken it upon herself to aggressively vie for position and power to gain respect during the second semester.

CONCLUSION

I have always been a minority and have fortunately learned how to successfully navigate my life. I respond to minority experiences daily without the opportunity to reflect on why or how I do what I do. The minority experience exercise has taught me the importance of reflection.

8

I Felt Like Everybody Else in the Church, and It Only Took One Person to Help Me, *and* Biracial and Double Minority

ARRON DECKARD

I was lucky enough to find out that there was an African American church no more than five minutes from my house. I've passed it many times before but had no idea that it was predominantly African American. I have to say that it was definitely an experience I wouldn't mind having again. The church had a medium-sized congregation, but it was small enough for me to meet a couple of people I will mention later on.

A DIFFERENT CHURCH

I don't normally attend church, but compared to the past churches that I have visited, this was completely different from predominantly white churches. There were several things that I noticed were different. One of the biggest differences is in the way music is played. In (white) churches I have been to, there has always been a band. They had guitarists, drummers, singers, and keyboardists. At AME, they had a choir, a keyboard player, and a drummer—that was it. Another observation I made was that one of the ministers was actually singing. In past churches I visited, they usually did not. Another aspect that I picked up on is that the keyboard player would softly play as the reverend was praying or when he was preaching. I liked this a lot because it added to the feeling. It helped to make the prayer more meaningful and sermon more powerful, which was already pretty moving. This stood out to me because in previous churches, it is typical for everybody to be quiet as the reverend delivers his sermon.

One last observation is that many people would actually talk during prayer. They would say phrases like "Mercy" or "Lord Jesus." This was different to me because just like I am used to complete silence during the sermon, I am also used to complete silence during prayer. People talking out loud and getting into the prayer was great. I found it really interesting as people would actually begin to cry during prayer. These were just a few observations that I wanted to point out during my visit to AME.

Personal Feelings: "Why Is He Here?"

Concerning the way I was feeling, well, that's a whole different story. When I first arrived at AME, I hesitated to get out of my car. I wasn't nervous because I'm uncomfortable being around African Americans; I was more nervous and anxious about being the only nonblack there. Even the night before, I had wondered if they would accept me, what questions they would ask, or if they would stare at me. To be honest, I was sort of a wreck. I arrived there around 10:45 A.M., and services started at 11:00 A.M., so I anxiously sat in the back corner of the room waiting for everything to begin. A little girl several rows ahead of me kept staring at me, and I heard her ask her mother, "Why is he here?" Luckily, the mother didn't turn around and just let her daughter continue on. I couldn't have felt any more lonely than I did at that moment. That was definitely one of the most significant and scariest feelings I had. The feeling of being lonely and the outcast was horrible. Sure, there were people around me, but if a little girl was asking why I was there, then I couldn't help but wonder what the adults were thinking. It was definitely an emotion I will never forget. As more people began showing up, I could see them shaking hands and hugging one another. People actually had friends to welcome them into the church. They all seemed to know each other, which only helped feed my feelings of loneliness.

During the service, several songs were played and sung before the reverend began his sermon—and I need to add that it was an amazingly powerful sermon; so much emotion was put into it. Not only did he keep me awake, but he kept me wanting to know more and to listen to him more intently. His style of preaching was completely opposite that of the past preachers I have heard. It was truly a great thing to experience.

Becoming a Part of the Church, Starting with One

Not long after the songs were over and the preaching had begun, a nice old woman sitting in front of me looked back at me and patted the seat beside her. My initial reaction was along the lines of "Who? Me?" I was confused at first, but then I realized she was telling me to sit beside her. It was a complete surprise to me, and I'm so glad she let me sit beside her and her granddaughter for the rest of the service. That pretty much eliminated that lonely feeling I was carrying in my mind. No longer was I the nonblack person in the church sitting alone, I was now part of the church and enjoying it with everybody else. On top of that, during the parts of the services where we were supposed to turn around and shake hands to meet people, I actually had people's hands to shake. It was awesome!

When the services ended, the nice lady introduced herself as Enid, and her granddaughter Jessica, and also said one thing that just made my whole day. She told me before I left, "If you come back next Sunday, you just come sit beside me so that you'll be comfortable." I couldn't believe it! That was probably the best feeling I had all day. I went from feeling so lonely to feeling so accepted, and it was an awesome transition. Enid was an amazingly nice woman, and her acceptance of me was one I won't forget. I no longer felt different—I felt equal. I felt like everybody else in the church, and it only took one person to help me.

BIRACIAL AND DOUBLE MINORITY

I have felt like a minority in a number of other situations. An interesting fact is that I am half white and half Chinese. Therefore, feeling like a minority can go both ways for me. An example of feeling like a "white" minority is when my family goes to authentic Chinese restaurants. Whenever we go to these restaurants, I cannot help but feel like a minority. My mother is full Chinese and can speak Mandarin, but I cannot. Sometimes I feel bad because I am half Chinese, yet I don't speak Mandarin. I don't feel "in touch" with my Asian roots when I am around "authentic" Chinese people.

My side of feeling like a Chinese minority, however, is more common. It was especially common in high school. I used to be teased and picked on for being Chinese. My eyes aren't as slanted as other Chinese kids' because I'm half white, but kids would act as if they were. They would crack jokes, asking me if I knew Bruce Lee, if I was good at karate, if I could speak Chinese, if we ate dogs and cats, and of course they had several names they came up with. My favorite was "lemon sucker." Although I did not think that these names and jokes hurt my feelings, they contributed to my shame of being a Chinese. I wanted to be full-white and not half-white.

I now know that it's a great thing to be culturally different because I think that makes people more interesting. I went from being ashamed of being Chinese to wanting to embrace it. In retrospect, the kids who picked on me only helped create my awareness that I am Chinese. Ultimately, it helped me become proud of my Chinese roots, and I am starting to embrace that side of me.

While my peers were picking on me in school, I never told the teacher, and I don't think that my teachers realized what was going on. I was never outright offended and would often joke back with them. Most of the people who picked on me were friends, but some weren't. I just brushed it off and tried my best to not let it get to me.

TEACHING IMPLICATIONS

As a teacher, I believe that one of the biggest things that I can do for my minority students will be to make them feel welcomed and equal. I do not want to have my students feel lonely in my classroom. That was a feeling I experienced at AME, and I believe that no student should have to feel that way. I am older and completely comfortable with myself, yet I still encountered that feeling. I can only imagine what it would be like for a student just entering high school. Middle and high school years are a fragile phase of life for any student because they are very tough to get through. With many students searching for who they are or what they want to become, I have to make sure that they are not negatively influenced.

Helping minority students feel proud about who they are is very important. I know that I wasn't proud to be half Chinese in school, and having that mind-set isn't good for anybody. Everybody should be proud of who they are and should not wish to be different. Making sure that all students are proud of who they are will also be important when helping them feel *equal* with all other students.

One thing that I want to be sure to look out for is the hidden curriculum. I want to make sure I am not indirectly teaching my students values or beliefs that are unfair or make students feel unequal or inferior to others. I will help my students feel a sense of unity and also know that I recognize and respect their cultures. Acknowledging their cultural heritage will be important when trying to understand my students and the actions they take. Acknowledging, respecting, and accepting all cultures will help *me* be successful in the classroom and will also help my students become successful.

FINAL THOUGHTS

Overall, this exercise was a great experience for me. I was hesitant at first, but I am very happy that I got to experience it. It helped me understand how my future students may feel in the classroom, and I will be able to relate to them. I met a nice woman who took me from being lonely to feeling accepted in a matter of seconds. The feeling I received from it was phenomenal, and I couldn't help but smile at her. It's great to know that there are people out there who are very accepting of others, no matter what differences may be present. In the midst of people who just stare and wonder about others who are different, there are those people who are willing to go out on a limb, introduce themselves, and make them feel welcome. Being accepted has never been more meaningful than it was for me that Sunday morning, and I want to share that feeling and experience with all the future students I teach.

III

THE MINORITY EXPERIENCE FROM THE PERSPECTIVE OF MEMBERS OF RACIAL MAJORITY

9

Comparing Experiencing the Minority Exercise to a War Zone Experience: A Soldier's Reflection, *and* Breaking Out in Cold Sweat in All-Women's Company

DANIEL BLANKTON

After reading the instructions for this assignment, I experienced extreme emotions of anticipation, nervousness, fear, and anxiety. I thought of the displacement that I may experience, the lack of acceptance, and the denial. I had mixed emotions about doing it: What would they expect? What would "they" expect from me? As a retired soldier, working in thirteen different countries and two tours of duties could not and did not prepare me the undertaking this "simple" assignment. I thought about my anticipation of my first day of college, but it did not compare. I thought about my entrance into a war zone, and it did not compare. One may think that there are no similarities, but I draw many. Entering the war zone, I had emotions of fear and anticipation, because my life was on the line. Yet these emotions did not compare to the fear of rejection that I felt before entering this place unknown to me. I had trained for years to enter areas of combat but received a mere month of cross-cultural instruction to enter a place of worship as the minority.

After visiting a black worship service, my eyes were opened to the cultural characteristics with which I battle on a daily basis in my classroom. On entering the church premises, I felt that the environment was inviting yet extremely uncomfortable for me—being the only Caucasian individual in the entire place. The sound level was above a comfortable level for me. It was approximately ten minutes before the beginning of the church service, yet the energy of the congregation was at a high level, a higher level than I had ever experienced prior to a worship service. There were loud conversations all around—an obvious difference from my regular church service, where personal conversations were held at a calm whisper or soft talk. I found this interesting; this is the same method of talking and conversation that I experience in the classroom and hallways in my high school. Not being stereotypical, I had drawn certain conclusions prior to this experience, but I now realized that many of the traits I saw in the teenagers were also presented here in their parents and even grandparents.

As the service began, I was called out and welcomed—alone! Well, it was obvious enough that I wasn't a part of the congregation. However, the simple idea of singling me out for welcome by the pastor sent a strong burning of solitude through my veins. As the singing began, I was uncomfortable, overwhelmed, intrigued, and very much surprised at the differences. After a few minutes of mentally settling in, however, I began to enjoy the atmosphere and the music, even though it was not the atmosphere of my choice. Then the preaching began.

After an hour of musical worship in which a series of events caught me off-guard, the bishop rose to speak. Already a much livelier crowd than I am used to, I was, by now, prepared to handle anything. The bishop began speaking slowly, which made it easy for me to understand. Then he got wound up, and not only could I not understand what he was saying, but I could hardly even hear him speaking, because of the noise from congregants cheering him on. I felt as if I was at a pep rally, rather than a worship service. It was apparent to me that they understood and enjoyed what he was saying. However, I couldn't agree or disagree with him because I had no idea what he was saying.

School Connections

The most uncomfortable moment in the service was when I looked around and not only was I the only white person in the house, but I was also the only person still in my seat, when I had to be standing. I had not worshipped in a manner that required this amount of standing, shouting, and movement. At this point, I was uncomfortable not because of their actions and methods of worship but because of my lack of knowledge. I felt as if I were expected to act in this manner, even though I was an outsider—and obviously not a part of my worship style. I took some mental notes of how my students must feel when they walk into an algebra class of which they are unfamiliar, are faced with difficult problems they have never seen before, and are surrounded by strangers who act and feel differently.

It would have been much easier for me to stand and act in the manner they were acting yet still be uncomfortable. I thought about how many of my students are probably "going through the motions" to just fit in. Sometimes the "motions" are coping mechanisms, some of which include good or bad behavior. The point, however, is that many students are just following the example of the crowds, even though they feel extremely uncomfortable.

As I reflected on my short experience, I realized that being the minority in the room was an issue not because I was white and they were black, but because I did not act or worship as they did. I felt extremely uncomfortable because I was not comfortable with their ways of worship. Consequently, the manner in which I conducted myself made me the minority in that room. Right or wrong, my actions or the lack thereof made me feel like the minority, not necessarily because of my race but because of my lack of contextual knowledge.

Even though the congregation at this church was extremely nice and considerate of my position, it was still uncomfortable walking into the new experience, and I blame myself for the conversations I did have. Because of the "fear of the unknown" I experienced—even before the service began—I cheated myself of conversations that I could have had, and I blame myself and only myself for depriving myself of potential valuable conversations.

BREAKING OUT IN COLD SWEAT IN AN ALL-WOMEN'S COMPANY

This is one incident I try not to bring up often due to the embarrassment factor involved. My wife was member of a ladies bingo night. Once a month, this group of about ten women moved around from one person's house to another to play bingo and have a night of fellowship. Well, the night finally arrived for the group to be at our house. Owing to a series of events, the meal my wife had planned to prepare fell through. Her misfortune turned to be my *extreme* misfortune or even my demise: I was elected to cook. What a situation I had found myself in! A houseful of twelve hungry women, with me as the only male in the house—an extreme minority.

With my new position as the minority, I felt just as strange walking into my own house full of women as I did walking into that church service described earlier. Not only out of place in my own house, but I was also cooking. Out of place and out of role, my obsession was to try and disappear into the back of the kitchen and finish the meal. I tried some lame jokes, pathetic conversations, and felt terribly out of place, weird, and extremely uncomfortable. Nothing really mattered except to finish my job there and disappear out the back door. Even though the ladies attempted to make me feel comfortable and did nothing to make me feel otherwise, I struggled to hide my cold sweat. They were supernice, friendly and offered assistance, yet I knew I was out of place, thus creating a very high level of adversity inside me.

Teaching Implications

The discomfort I felt even when the ladies strived to make me feel welcome was a vital point that will change the activities in my classroom. Even though I was in a familiar place, I was still uncomfortable with my surroundings and *could not perform.* I struggled to even be myself. I finished the meal in about forty-five minutes and out the back door I went! It was such a relief to leave the house even though no one there was creating turmoil for me. I was uncomfortable, and it didn't matter what their actions were: the mood was all in my mind. I was out of place, and the ladies' actions could not fix that problem even though they made noble attempts.

During my second semester of teaching, I had an ESL student, Maria, from Puerto Rico. She could barely speak English and felt clueless in school. This child was lost. I never realized how much her displacement impacted her life until I began reflecting on the minority experience. Maria struggled through the semester to keep her straight A average but did so with extremely hard work. I thought that she was shy and reserved, but I now believe that she was going through the minority experience. I now understand the position she took and the disposition she held through my classes.

I only spent a few hours during my uncomfortable situations, and they warped me for hours. Therefore, I could not imagine students revisiting these experiences on a daily basis and still be expected to perform well.

FINAL THOUGHTS AND PLAN OF ACTION FOR TEACHING

Being a majority most of my life, I have taken for granted the comfortable feeling that I enjoy in everyday situations. In most situations, I have a feeling of security, confidence, and normalcy that I now realize most of my students do not have. I have tried to imagine myself as a fifteen-year-old minority student in a new school, with new people, experiencing these overwhelming situations, and it is a tough situation. As a teacher, this reflection brings me to a humble state of intense planning in ways that can make the transition for all students easier, especially for minority students who have higher hurdles to clear.

As a classroom teacher, I plan to lower the walls of cultural differences. I will ensure that my classroom decorations do not project a male-dominated atmosphere. I will try to ensure that the females are comfortable. I will strive to mix gender-neutral activities early in the semester to cross-train the students.

This exercise has helped me to learn some cultural characteristics that could influence the learning styles and attributes different students possess. I plan to implement a class exercise whereby I collect information about each student, their abbreviated history and background information, and how their particular cultural backgrounds could facilitate my work with them. I will plan activities for the first two weeks of class to mix the students from different cultural backgrounds and teach them about one another. This would not necessarily help the students learn algebra—directly—but it would help the minority students to be more comfortable in my classroom and therefore perform better. In the past, I have tried to foster classroom–community relationships, and I think that this attempt to learn about one another's culture will enhance this effort by increasing the understanding of their culture-based actions.

10

I Already Felt Unwelcome, and . . . This Feeling Was Completely Inside My Head, *and* Stuttering at a Staff Meeting

Ryan Delehant

I want to begin by saying this was one of the most interesting and difficult experiences I have ever had in my life. I love to learn new things no matter what they are, in order to find new information and understanding of different things. Besides, learning about people is something that really drives me. With that said, I viewed this activity as a great opportunity to help me understand a large portion of the student body that I deal with on a regular basis—and it was such an opportunity. The only problem was the fact that I am a relatively shy person and can easily feel out of place in any group of people I do not know, especially in a culturally shocking setting.

I was not raised in a family that regularly attended church, so I generally feel uneasy in religious settings. Notwithstanding the fact that this was an extremely difficult, emotionally trying experience, I feel it was worth it in the long run. I feel that I have a better understanding of the feeling of uneasiness that comes with being the minority in a situation and how it feels to be left out and not welcome.

I chose to attend an African American church close to the school where I am currently teaching for two main reasons. First, the students I seem to have the most difficulty relating to and have the most discipline problems with are my African American male students. Second, the African American population is the largest minority population in my current school. Therefore, I felt that I would have the most to benefit from this experience by going to this church in order to learn how to work with my students on a daily basis.

GOING TO CHURCH

As soon as I arrived at the church, I began feeling very uneasy and apprehensive about the experience that was about to happen. Before I even came in contact with any members of the congregation, I already felt unwelcome, and it had nothing to do with the members of the church: this feeling was completely inside my head. I was extremely nervous and, to a certain extent, almost afraid because I suddenly felt that I had no idea what I was going to encounter. As I was approaching the church, I noticed some members around the front who were engaged in conversation in what I would consider a very loud and boisterous tone. My presence caught almost everyone's attention. As I approached closer to them, I noticed that some were staring at me while others broke into a very hushed conversation. A few of the members made eye contact with me and greeted me with a head nod, and another member said "Hello" to me.

I entered the church building and found a seat in the back—relatively by myself. I did this completely subconsciously and was sitting by myself in the last pew before I even realized that I was inside the church! I arrived very close to the start of the church service, so it started only a few minutes after I sat down. People filed in the church shortly after I sat down, and I do not believe any person missed me as I sat in the last pew. When the service started, I immediately noticed that this service was going to be completely different from any church service I had been to before. Although I did not regularly attend church as a child, when I did, it was a Christian church service. Sometimes, I go to church with my girlfriend at a "progressive" Christian church with a very upbeat tempo. This service today, however, started off very loud and animated. Members were up out of their seats dancing and singing very energetically. One could see the spiritual energy within all the members—old and young—and they were very expressive of their feelings. It was very different from anything I have ever experienced in a church before, but I have to say it was very exhilarating.

When the pastor started preaching, the congregation was not as loud, but they were very affirming, saying "Amen" and other things to let him know they agreed with what he was saying. During the prayer, the entire church was silent, and it was an amazing change—very sudden. One minute the church was vibrant and full of life, and then it was completely silent! Interestingly, the actual church service was started and completed in what seemed like just minutes to me.

All by Myself!

Once the service was over, everyone started to leave the church building, amid loud conversations. This was a dramatic change for me because during the church service, I felt like I was almost forgotten, although I also felt simultaneously that many eyes were on me. At this point, however, I felt that *everyone* was staring directly at me, almost as if asking, "What is he doing here?" I felt extremely uncomfortable at this point. I suddenly wanted to be out of this situation as quickly as possible. I shuffled into the crowd and exited the church quickly. Once outside, I did linger in front of the church for a little while. However, I was unable to bring myself to attempt to engage with any of the members as they stood in front of the church in conversation. After a few minutes of trying to work up the courage to go talk to someone, I gave up, went to my car, and left the church premises.

Some Reflections

Being the minority in the church was something that I had never truly felt before. I grew up in a very isolated community with very few African Americans. There was a relatively large Hispanic population, but my high school did not even have a single African American student until my senior year. Being the minority in any situation is something almost completely new to me. Therefore, my experience was eye-opening. I never thought that an uneasy feeling could be that strong. When the church service ended and I felt that every eye was on me, the uneasy feeling almost made me nauseous. The whole experience left me with an amazingly uneasy feeling. I felt that everyone was looking at me and saying that I was not wanted there, although that was in direct opposition to the demeanor that most of the members had shown toward me when they addressed me. No one was rude toward me, and most of the members I made eye contact or exchanged pleasantries with were very welcoming. Basically, there was a fear of the unknown in me, and that made me uneasy throughout the entire experience. It was a very powerful feeling that made me feel like I was out of place and was not supposed to be there.

As already indicated, unfortunately, I was unable to overcome this uneasy feeling in order to make contact with any members of the congregation beyond a simple "Hi" or "Hello." They were friendly, but no one attempted to make conversation with me, and there were a few members that simply stared in my general direction and held hushed conversations. These were the members of the congregation who made me feel very unwelcome.

I think that the biggest surprise of the entire experience was the church service itself. I have the idea that a congregation sits quietly and listens to the message from the preacher. In this setting, the congregation noisily affirmed the message the preacher was conveying. It was very different for me because this behavior in the churches I am familiar with would probably be seen as very disrespectful.

STUTTERING AT A STAFF MEETING

Another experience that compares to this one of being the minority in a public situation would be the first schoolwide meeting I ever attended at my school. From my high school graduation, I have known that I wanted to be a math teacher. I started my college education at the community college for the first two years. When I transferred to a four-year college and learned about the amount of extra time required to graduate with my math degree as well as my education degree, I opted to go the route of lateral entry to become a teacher. When I got my first teaching job, I had never been in a classroom as an authority figure. I had just graduated with my undergraduate degree in mathematics and still considered myself a kid.

The first full staff meeting was a very scary experience. I only knew two or three other teachers at the school, other than the administrative staff who had hired me. I was therefore very uneasy and apprehensive; I felt like a student who was somewhere I should not be. Everyone was in loud conversation, and I felt like everyone looked at me when I entered. I was welcomed by one of the teachers I did know; she saw me enter and invited me to sit with her during the meeting.

At one point during the meeting, I was asked to introduce myself to the staff. I stuttered and spoke extremely poorly. If I could have seen myself, I am sure that I was as red as the inside of a watermelon. From that point of the meeting, I felt like everyone was looking and talking about me, saying, "What's this 'kid' doing here? He cannot be a teacher!" Fortunately for me, my nervousness from this experience had little to no consequence. In retrospect, no one at the meeting was probably talking about me, and now that I have gone to a few more staff meetings, I think that over half the teachers there were probably not paying the least bit of attention to me. I was able to recover from this situation, although I still do not feel completely comfortable around the "older" group of teachers in my school. I have formed many bonds with some of the younger as well as new teachers in the school.

REMEMBERING JOHNNY

For some students, the position of being the minority sometimes has dramatic and long-lasting effects on their educational experiences. One such situation happened this year in one of my Technical Mathematics I classes during the first semester. This class section was very small, with only eighteen students. Johnny was one of the only two African American male students in this class. Another factor that made this student the minority in the class was the fact he was the only junior in the entire class; everyone else was a sophomore or senior. He seemed like he knew no one in the class, and right from the first day of class, he was immediately withdrawn. He sat down in the back of the room and spoke to no one. This continued for the entire first week of class. He did all his work perfectly, he and the other black student were always on time, and he was never a class disruption; he just never spoke to anyone in the class and rarely contributed during class discussion.

I always welcomed him and talked to him when he arrived for class, but he seemed very uneasy in my class and never really opened up. Eventually, he started to struggle with his class work and his grades fell. He started missing days and never asked what material he had missed or how to make up the daily quizzes and class work for those days. He ended up passing the class with a C. I was never able to break the ice with him and really get him to open up during my class. I know that he was a bright student and had the ability to achieve a much higher grade in my class than he actually did.

TEACHING IMPLICATIONS

A reflection on this and other students' experiences in my classroom has led me to believe that the consequences of being the minority can be an extremely damaging force to a student's education. Being uneasy and apprehensive all the time at school could easily lead to students dropping out or just simply not coming to school at all. We, as teachers, have to do whatever we can to help combat this experience. Although we will not be able to make them feel like they are not the minority completely, we can attempt to do things to minimize the effects.

I can help combat the minority experience in my own classroom by spending some time to really understand the culture of the minority students in my class. I could drive around the area of my school in order to understand the type of neighborhoods my students come from. I can research the historical figures and heroes of the minority students in my classroom, and attend some cultural activities of the students in my classroom. In effect, I can make an attempt to really see what is important in my minority students' lives.

I also need to try to better understand both the verbal and nonverbal communications that are the norm of different cultures by doing research and observations. I feel that this is probably one of the most important things for me to address immediately. Some of the most troubling issues I have in my classroom come from my African American male students. Many times, I ask myself, "What did I do wrong to make that student act that way?" When reflecting on the situations that occur in my classroom, I often wonder how much of it derives from my not really understanding how to deal with these students. I am a very demanding, stern teacher for my students. I expect them to do the things I ask them without having to justify them. I feel that they should know I am there to help them and that the things that I am asking them to do are for their benefit. Maybe if I, as the teacher, handled them a little bit differently, they would have reacted differently to me. I know that there is no quick answer because every student is different and one has to learn how to work with all students in order to be a successful teacher.

The one quick change I would make right now is to really work at making my minority students feel welcome. I need to make an effort to connect with all of my students, especially the minority students I tend to struggle with. The crippling effects of experiencing being the minority must be minimized to ensure the success of all students in all classes.

We need to be aware that experiencing the minority is not limited to the normal situations that immediately come to mind, such as skin color or the language we speak. It can be almost anything. We never know what could make a person feel out of place and apprehensive in a group of people. Therefore, all teachers need to make all students feel welcome from the minute they enter their classroom. Every student has the right to learn and should not feel like they have nothing to contribute just because they are different. The fact that they are different could be just the very reason why the things they have to say could be insightful and important!

11

Getting a "Good Seat" at Granite, *and* A Different Worldview, a Different Life

STEPHANIE JOHNSTON

I visited Granite AME Zion Church early one Sunday morning. As I walked in, I heard a choir and assumed they were practicing; they were actually just singing and enjoying it as others filed into the church. I was greeted by an elderly man who alerted a young woman of my presence as a visitor, and she pointed out a "good seat." For me, it was hard to hear enough to talk to others over the noise, but no one else seemed to have an issue. The sanctuary was abuzz with church members' fellowshipping with one another, passing babies around, and getting their "Sunday hugs." All people in attendance had on their "Sunday best." I had been warned by an African American coworker that I should dress nicely for the visit because "black people believe in Sunday clothes." She was right; there was an array of big hats, frilly dresses, and even real flowers tucked into men's coat pockets.

When the choir sang to officially begin the service, they stood, and I noticed their robes. They were beautiful and trimmed in gold and looked very hot. When the organ began, like clockwork, the choir members began to sway in unison.

As one of three white people in the room, I felt totally awkward. The other white people in attendance were obviously girlfriends of black church members; they seemed to fit in, although they were slightly more subdued. I wanted to know what they thought of my visiting and even thought of something I could tell them if they asked. I was afraid they were going to think I was coming in to spy or pass judgment.

Connections

I felt welcome in the service and more *unnoticed* than I had imagined being. I had imagined the entire congregation staring and whispering about my presence, but that did not happen. A total of five women and one man greeted me prior to the service; I shook hands with virtually every member present during the "handshaking song." Although I had interaction with most people there, I feel like I only connected meaningfully with the pastor and his wife. I do not think it was because I was not receptive to connections; I think the folks there were used to their routine and paid little attention to my company. This was another meaningful realization in comparison with behaviors toward minorities in the classroom.

Surprises and Insights about My Students

The biggest surprise for me was realizing how uncomfortable I felt during the experience. I work with African American teachers and students and have black relatives who have married into my family, yet I was extremely anxious about being the only one like me in the church. The only thing really unique about me was my skin color. I speak the same language, I live in the same community, and our families frequent the same schools and businesses. However, in the moment, I was not able to find much commonality with any of the people there. I just felt different and lonely and even sad at times. I am somewhat ashamed of the way I felt, embarrassed that the experience was not as easy as I had thought or hoped it would be.

Another surprise was how connected I felt with my minority students after attending the service. When I was conflicted about raising my hands in praise during the service, I felt that must be the kind of choices my students make on a regular basis. They must have moments where they choose to participate in activities in order not to stick out or offend others. The feelings of sadness for me came from missing my own church. I missed our graduation Sunday to attend the minority church, and I was really saddened by that. My minority students must feel the same when we do little to recognize important holidays in their culture such as Ramadan or Day of the Dead. They miss important cultural events, and we do not even know about it.

A DIFFERENT WORLDVIEW, A DIFFERENT LIFE

The most interesting minority situation I recall observing did not happen in my classroom at school. It occurred in my classroom at church. As a youth leader, I deal with similar situations at school and at church in relation to cultural diversity. The issues seem to be easier to recognize and deal with at church since the setting is more intimate and the relationships are much deeper.

When I started working at church, I had a homeschooled child, Michelle, in my youth group, and she stuck out like a sore thumb in every social situation we encountered. She had lived a very sheltered life and did not connect with many of the others in the youth group. Her parents were overly strict and would let her participate in only select activities that I planned for the group. Getting permission for her to go on overnight trips took extra plans and extra chaperones. The others in the group noticed, and a few immature boys even picked on her on occasion. I made sure the teasing was controlled, although it never seemed to bother Michelle. In fact, Michelle thought herself to be superior to the others in the group. I attributed this attitude to her perception regarding the public school system as a den for mischievous acts.

Strain and Stress

Michelle's overall outlook on her position as the minority and my position as a proponent of the "majority" paradigm made our interactions strained and stressful. I was a public school teacher and easily related to the other students in the youth group. She had little in common with any of the others and was proud of it. When others discussed their school lives, good and bad, she would either look down her nose on them or be totally confused by their situation. She regularly commented, ". . . and that is why I am not going to public school," a remark I resented more as time went on.

The stance of superiority from her parents made it difficult to address the situation in the way I would have liked. In any other situation where a student behaves in a superior manner, I would address the situation directly and move on. I had to handle this one with kid gloves because I did not want her parents to feel as though I was going against their teaching at home or discouraging her coming to youth group altogether. Eventually, Michelle made the choice herself to limit her attendance, based on the level of activity the event included. For example, she never missed a fund-raiser, but she never went on a trip to an amusement park. Unlike most of my public school students, she did not feel the need to be entertained; however, she felt the need to be of service. I knew from conversations with her that her school day at home included a lengthy list of chores to be done before school could be out. This must account for her willingness to work and serve others at the church.

Although she was extremely helpful at times, I honestly had a hard time treating Michelle equally in light of the situation. I wanted to make her realize what she was missing as a homeschooled student. I am ashamed to say that I was tempted to rub in her face the fun of football games and passing notes in the hall. I firmly believed and still believe that she lacked a great deal of socialization skills and basic communication skills that are fostered in a public school setting. I wanted her to conform and fit in with the group, even though she was comfortable with who she was and the education she was receiving.

Reflections

Looking back, I believe that Michelle's superior attitude was a defense mechanism. She probably did want to fit in but knew that she had no chance of being a normal student. She resisted the interests of others in the group because they were such foreign concepts to her. Since she was a very bright student, she must have realized that her parents would never allow her to behave in the way that the others did, so to ease the difficulty of the situation, she became turned off and was almost offended by normal teenage behavior.

The consequence of Michelle's minority experience was that her parents eventually left the church and began participating in a new trend of "home churching." It is the ultimate form of isolation from the outside world. Although she is in college now, she takes all of her classes online and works at her family's company with her siblings. Michelle is now an adult and has never been away from home for more than a couple of nights. She has never been on a date, maybe never even had a crush. All the things I was afraid would happen for her have happened. She is no longer a sheltered teenager; she is a sheltered adult. The situation is very sad to me because I had held hope for a brief time that I might be able to be an agent of change for her. I think, however, that it might have been possible, had my attitude been different at the time.

CONCLUSION

The Experiencing the Minority exercise was very eye-opening for me as a teacher. Although I feel as though I only got a small taste of what my minority students feel like in my classroom, I have been motivated to change my classroom practices in order to reach out to them more.

If I could make any changes right now to promote a healthier minority experience, I would begin educating the teachers. This would help entire schools to be minority-friendly places. I think that teachers need to have more education about the type of students we work with. It is easy to think, "I have twenty white students, four black students, and three Latinos" and stop there, without understanding what these demographics imply. That is the attitude I would like to change, and I think it is going to take more education to do it. In my school, we have weekly "focus meetings" during our planning period when we are supposed to be educated on useful teaching strategies. I would like to see one day a month devoted to education about the diversity inside our classrooms. It takes time to learn about and thus appreciate *others* for their uniqueness, but it is worth it.

12

Experiencing the Minority at a Hip-Hop Dance Class, *and* A Good-Kid-Turned-Bad: Surviving Black History Month

Karlie Kissman

For my Experience the Minority project, I chose to attend a dance class in inner-city Charlotte. I chose a hip-hop class that was made up of mostly African Americans. I chose this because it relates to my content as well as the project. I researched the studio through the Internet and word of mouth so that I knew I would be the minority in the class.

When I arrived at the studio, there were groups of people waiting in the lobby. I went in alone and headed straight to the receptionist's desk. While walking between a few groups of people to get there, I felt as if all eyes were on me. I was wondering what they were thinking. "Who is she?" "What is she doing here?" "Is she in the wrong place?" These and many other questions were racing through my mind. I realized later that they just as easily could have been paying no attention to me, but as self-centered humans, we assume differently in these situations.

I proceeded to tell the girl behind the counter that I was there for the 8:15 hip-hop class. She quickly responded, "Ten dollars." During the transaction, I felt that I was still being watched. I do not know if anyone was even paying any attention to me, but I still felt that all eyes were on me. I began feeling slightly anxious and nervous.

Managing My Nerves

After fumbling with my money and handing it to the girl, I waited for her to tell me where to go or what to do next. She said nothing. Before I had a chance to ask her, she was back into her conversation with a friend standing at the other end of the counter. I collected my things and quickly found the closest open area against a waiting room wall. Instead of asking someone if they were all waiting for the 8:15 class and making myself more uncomfortable, I assumed that they were and kept to myself. I had arrived about ten minutes early so that I would not be late. I was now wishing that I had arrived exactly on time to avoid awkwardness. While waiting, I changed my shoes, stretched, and checked my cell phone to avoid looking out of place. I assumed that if you look busy, people will generally leave you alone.

Dance Time

Just a few minutes later, the studio door opened and the previous class came filing out. There were a few other Caucasian females in that class, but I was the only one in the waiting room for the following class. After the line of people coming out ended, a few people in the waiting room began gathering their belongings and headed toward the studio. I quickly did the same. Typically, I love to be in the front row of dance classes so that I can be sure to see the teacher and have the most room possible. In this place, however, I found myself making my way to the back corner since I was unsure of how the class operated. The teacher in the front of the room was also a male African American.

Once the class began, I felt a little more comfortable, considering dance is my artistic and emotional outlet. I watched the other people in the class closely as it went on. I noticed that they tended to be more outspoken, fun, lively and playful than students in classes that I am used to. The teacher was very attentive to everyone in the class and showed no signs of favoritism, including attention to little me in the back corner. He checked in with me occasionally to make sure I was following along well.

Connections and Reflections

As the class ended, a few of the people standing close to me began a casual conversation with each other and me. They talked about the workout and how they will try it again next week. Other people in the room stuck around after class for a few minutes to "free dance" and play around with the teacher and each other. I gathered my things and headed out after thanking the instructor.

From my observations of the people in the class, I think that they definitely fit into the cultural elements of African Americans. They were expressive, vocal, and free with their movement. They called out to each other during class, encouraging one another to try new movements and often included *their own* movements into the class. All of these things made the class very interesting, exciting and unpredictable. It was very different from the very strict style of dance classes that I am accustomed to. Surprisingly, though, none of these elements disrupted the flow of the class or the material the teacher was presenting. Everyone was very respectful, and the teacher was able to get through all of the material he had prepared for class.

Being the minority in the room began as a very uncomfortable feeling. It caused me to focus a lot of my attention on myself and not on the dance material being presented. I did calm down and relax a little as the class went on, but my minority situation continued to stick in the back of my head.

Because of my uncomfortable feeling, I was not very successful in engaging with others in the room. I did connect with two others in some quick casual conversation at the end of class, but that was the extent of it. The group appeared to be very cordial with one another. There were a lot of loud conversations, private conversations, laughter, and more. I did not find the group to be rude or ignoring me, but they were less cordial to me. I did not assume this was because I was the minority but because they simply did not know me.

Conclusion

The experience went fairly close to how I expected it to go. I did not come across any major surprises, although I did not expect to be quite so nervous. I thought that I would feel a little more comfortable because the setting was a dance studio. I realized that being the minority (the only Caucasian) in the class caused me a lot of anxiety and took so much of my cognition away from what I wanted to focus it on: dance.

A GOOD-KID-TURNED-BAD: SURVIVING BLACK HISTORY MONTH

The public high school that I attended was probably 98 percent white. There was one black male who took a few of the same classes as me. I remember having special assignments in class during Black History Month. I thought that a black student who was very proud of and comfortable with his background would be excited to do these activities. Conversely, this was not that student. He was typically somewhat outgoing and friendly. During these special activities, however, he became more quiet and not as good a student. He often missed classes during this time, acted out inappropriately, and did not hand in work. When he was there, he was very quiet during class discussions and activities. I also noticed him acting as though he had no interest in the material or the history of African Americans.

Black History Month as a Point of Differentiation

Before the Black History Month and even more so after, this student was identified by others as a "white boy." To many, he did not fit the mold of a teenage African American. As a culturally proficient teacher, I see so much more in the behaviors of this student. He did not feel comfortable addressing a serious issue that secluded him from the other students. If African American history had been appropriately incorporated into the entire school year, it may not have been as threatening to him. As the minority, he probably wanted to blend with the other students as much as possible. Creating an entire month of special activities and lessons that blatantly separates him from others must have been overwhelming and nerve-racking for him. I can only imagine how he felt when discussing these issues: all eyes were on him, whether he liked it or not. He must have felt that he was being differentiated from everyone else.

During Black History Month, although it is possible for some students to find this as their time to tell stories and shine, others may see it as a means of segregation from the larger group. The result of Black History Month for this student was not beneficial. It caused him to shut down and act out negatively.

REFLECTIONS

As an adult, I was uncomfortable when placed in a situation where I was the minority. The feelings I experienced were challenging. This project truly made me take a deep look at the effects being a minority student could have on a child. Many students deal with these issues every single day at school and even in their communities. I can see how their attention and focus can easily veer away from the material a teacher is providing them. Their cognitive resources become limited because they have much more to learn and cope with. These children may also evolve new personalities that are coping mechanisms that they feel will protect them from discrimination. They are often managing their cultures, new cultural norms, friends, family, school work, teachers, jobs and much more in the same phase of life. All of these things combined would be challenging for even adults to sort out. Children in such challenging situations may therefore use much more of their cognitive resources to resolve such issues, instead of focusing on their school work.

SOLUTIONS AND CONCLUSION

In my opinion, the first step for helping minority students to feel more comfortable is to make the curriculum culturally diverse. Focusing one week or month on other cultures is not enough. The curriculum needs to be thoroughly integrated. This will allow students to feel more included on a day-to-day basis. Teachers also need to make the effort to learn about their students and especially their diverse learners. This will help them to create a more comfortable learning environment.

The Experience the Minority project forced me to look deeper into what it means to be the minority. As a white female in this country, it is not something that I typically deal with. If you have never experienced something first-hand, it makes it very hard to understand. After completing the project, I realize what it means to be the minority. I am glad that I spent just one hour experiencing it, but I also recognize that this experience pales in comparison to people who deal with it every single day. Diverse learners need to be understood by teachers so that we can help them achieve their highest potential. In the future, I hope to find myself (purposefully or not) in more situations where I am the minority so that I can continue learning about these students and the challenges they face every day.

13

A German's Visit to a Latino Church, *and* German Sensibilities at a Super Bowl Party

ANGELA JAKEWAY

I come from another country with a different language and a different culture. I have an American husband, so we have diversity even at home. In Germany, we had people with other cultures living around us, mostly from Spain, Italy, Greece, and Turkey. For my minority experience, I chose to go to a Hispanic church service. I don't speak Spanish, and I am not used to going to church alone, so I was nervous going there because I did not know what to expect.

When I pulled into the parking lot, I saw that the church was huge. It was very different from the churches I am used to, which are all older and much smaller. I saw many people going to the big entrance. I followed them, and as soon as I came to the entrance, I recognized that this was not the service I was supposed to go to: This was the regular service in English. I asked for the Hispanic service.

After I found my way around, I saw a small building behind the huge church building. When I entered the building, I immediately felt like I was in a different world. I attend a German church, where everybody looks for a place to sit next to their family members and quietly waits for the service to start. In this new church, all the people were standing around and talking loudly to each other. It even seemed like some were fighting. People were dressed in very dressy, colorful clothes. The children were running around laughing and having fun. To me, this was like being in a different world. German church congregants are always dressed in black and white clothing. Children keep close to their parents quietly and wait for the adults to finish their greetings.

When I walked in, people looked at me with surprise, and I very quickly looked for a seat in the back row. There were no singing books or Bibles in the rows—which you would find in a German church. The members came to church with Bibles nicely wrapped in book covers.

When the service started, I didn't understand a word. Half of the service was singing in Spanish. There were monitors which showed the Spanish words. This helped me to follow along. I could also follow some of the prayers, because they sounded like some of mine from my church.

Throughout the entire service I felt very uncomfortable and lonely. I almost felt like I had left my family. I know going to a church should not be about going with your family. However, I have been a mother for thirteen years, and if I do anything without my children, I feel like I have done something wrong. Therefore, I felt like I was neglecting them, by being here all alone.

The entire service was much different. In the German service people sing very quietly, because they are quiet in their basic life. In this service, in contrast, everybody seemed to know all the words, and everybody, whether they were good singers or not, sang loudly. I remained very quiet. The songs were very modern, and the people raised their arms while singing. Fortunately, the last part of the service was done in English and Spanish. I loved this, because I could finally be a part of that service.

After I sat down, I looked around more, and I recognized much more color. I had black pants on with a white-and-black blouse and only a little bit of makeup. My shoes were with a small heel and very comfortable. The other women had much more makeup, high heels, and colorful dresses. I felt wrongly dressed and out of place.

When the service was over, I tried to talk to some of the people in the church. They were nice to me; however, we had difficulties in communicating. I have a German accent, and they had a Spanish accent, so the combination wasn't good for communication. They were very friendly, but I felt very misplaced and had the strong wish to go home to my family.

Some Reflections

Parts of the Hispanic service were shocking experiences for me. I had thought that I knew what it feels like to be alone. I grew up with no father and got married later than many of my friends. I lived alone for many years, and since my husband travels a lot because of his job, I was used to being alone more than many women I know, but this situation was very different. If I spoke Spanish, I could have understood the service and participated more in it. I could have also interacted more with them. Although they all seemed very nice, it was difficult to communicate who I was and what I do: "small talk" is the start of many relationships. I was also not dressed to fit in. This added to my discomfort. Going to a place where you don't know anybody is bad, but it is worse if you don't blend in.

All said, however, going alone to the Hispanic service was a good experience for life. It was an eye-opener for understanding cultural differences. I thought that because I am a foreigner (and "diverse"), I know what it is like to be different. I know a lot about German and American cultures, but I realized that I don't know a lot about other cultures. It was a great experience for going into a classroom where I will have diverse learners.

GERMAN SENSIBILITIES AT A SUPER BOWL PARTY

When I moved from Germany to the United States, there were many situations in which I felt as the minority. This has nothing to do with gender or skin color; it has to do with growing up in a different country. If you think about Germany, you may think it is similar to America, especially since many immigrants came from Germany. However, I felt very different when I went to my first Super Bowl party.

One year, when the Carolina Panthers made it to the Super Bowl, one family in my neighborhood had a Super Bowl party. Every neighbor was invited. My children and my husband wanted to go very badly, because they are all Panthers fans. So we went. When we arrived, I noticed the huge TV screen in the living room. I had never seen such a big TV. When we moved from Germany to the United States, we decided not to replace our televisions. In Germany, we have 220 volts, and everything that works only with electricity we had to leave behind in Germany and purchase anew, since in the United States, we use 120 volts instead. We replaced several things but decided to go with no TV in our house, located in a midsized town.

Misplaced and Bewildered

On seeing the large television, my first impression was, "Wow, everything is much bigger here in the United States!" We greeted the people from our neighborhood and walked around to talk with every single person. Soon, my husband disappeared into the living room toward the huge TV. Well, I thought we had come to watch the Super Bowl game, so I followed him. When I sat next to him, I looked around and only saw the men from our neighborhood and no women. I felt very much displaced and began wondering where the women were. I stood up, walked around, and found them all in the kitchen. They didn't even want to watch the game. Instead, they had come to talk about the goings-on in town. I was very surprised.

Even though this was the group I obviously fit into, I felt lonely. I didn't know any gossip, and I didn't watch TV, so I didn't know any shows. I started to look for my children. I found them in the children's room with computer games. They looked very astonished because we didn't have any computer games in our house. They, too, didn't know if they fit into this group.

I went to my husband and asked him if he could spend some time with me in the kitchen. Being a loving and understanding man, he agreed and did so. As he came closer, he saw many other neighbors walking into the garage. He went to check out what was going on. When he came back, he asked me if I wanted to have something from the *keg*. I got upset and told him that he should know better—I don't eat cake. He laughed out loud. I had misunderstood the pronunciation completely. I was thinking that they had a cake in the garage. He explained to me what a "keg" is and tried to teach me the correct pronunciation. I am not sure if I can pronounce this word even today. However, I know what it means, just in case.

Concluding Thoughts

My family had come to a party to watch the game and have fun. Sadly, I got bored. Since our children had to go to school the next day and we think it is very important that children have a good night's sleep, I decided to go home earlier. I wasn't sad to leave the party; I felt like this was the right decision. I could not have a good conversation because I wasn't very good in English, and I didn't know anything about what was going on in the TV shows the women were talking about.

Based on my experience, I decided not to go to a Super Bowl party again. I don't think it is bad to have such party, but I am not interested in it. We also got a TV at home. We decided that we should watch at least a little bit of TV, so we don't feel completely out of touch with the world. My husband can now watch some football games at home, and my son now plays football on a computer game and as a sport after school. I understand football more now, which makes my husband and son happy. If the Carolina Panthers make it to the Super Bowl again, I may have a party in my house, with the advantage that I can also sit with the men and watch the game.

14

Understanding My Students at Church, *and* Finding My Feet at My In-Laws'

JIM CROSS

I had no idea where to find a minority church or what to expect, so I approached an African American friend for some advice on the matter. I have not attended church since childhood, so I was very anxious about doing this exercise.

Come Sunday morning, I was surprised how nervous I felt while dressing for church. My mind was flooded with reasons to delay this exercise. When I arrived at the church, I was shocked and unnerved. Universal Church was the largest church I had ever witnessed. I parked and watched families as they arrived. They were all African American. I followed a large family to the entrance. I was warmly greeted by a large woman wearing bright colors and a huge smile. That gesture seemed sincere and helped calm me down. I sat at the end of a pew next to a older couple. They seemed oblivious to me.

The decor of the church seemed to be a nice mix of modern and traditional. There were three separate sections of pews with purple cushions and a balcony above. Upbeat, jazzy-type music filled the enormous room from electric keyboards. At the front of the sanctuary was a large glass podium surrounded by flowers. The choir loft was clearly visible behind the podium. I was surprised to see two television cameras stationed in the middle aisle. A large movie screen hung on one of the front walls. This was used for showing announcements and displaying song lyrics.

Relating the Experience to the Cultural Elements of African Americans

The service was loud, rhythmic, and involved a lot of motion. The songs were joyous and upbeat. The congregation clapped, snapped their fingers, and swayed to the beat without inhibition. Throughout the service, people nodded and voiced out their agreement with the pastor. Rhetorical questions were being answered as if the pastor were talking directly to each congregation member. These behaviors would seem to coincide with strong musical, rhythmic, and communicative aspects of the black culture.

I also noticed that many people were arriving well after the service had begun. They showed no apparent signs of embarrassment. The service seemed to be designed to take this into account. We were on our feet singing for the entire first thirty minutes. After the service, church members were social with each other and seemed to be in no hurry to leave. These observations seem to be reflective of this culture's concept of time: Time was "walking" slowly.

As a white person, sitting in close proximity to someone I did not know made me feel claustrophobic. However, my African American counterparts seemed to be very comfortable. There were times during the service when we were told to take the hand of the person next to us. The older lady next to me smiled and took my hand without hesitation. This was very uncomfortable for me. It seemed obvious that the African American culture has a smaller "personal distance" than what I am used to.

How I Felt Being the Minority in the Church

I absolutely did not like being in the minority at this church. Not only did I feel like a racial minority, but I also felt like a religious minority. All the people around me shared a belief that I did not. I felt guilty being in this place of worship for the sole purpose of learning what it is like to feel like a minority. My stomach was in knots, and I felt like everyone was looking at me. I could not wait to leave.

My Attempts at Engaging the Members of the Congregation

At one point in the service, the congregation was told to "greet and embrace" the ones around them. I recalled doing this at church when I was young. I remembered quick little handshakes to the right and the left. This is not what happened at this church. People all around me introduced themselves and wanted to know my name. This ritual lasted at least five minutes, and people actually left their pews to greet their friends sitting away from them. The truth is that the people around me were successful engaging with me, but I did not feel successful engaging with them. My throat was dry, and my voice cracked. I stumbled over my words and appeared very uncomfortable.

I did manage to have a reasonable conversation with a student and her parents after the service. Anna was in my class last year. She is a nice girl but did not pass my class. She called my name as I was trying to escape my minority experience. She asked me to return and meet her parents. I had communicated with her parents by phone previously, but I had never actually met them. While I had my "teacher hat" on, I was much more comfortable conversing. You might expect that these folks would have been upset or at least uncomfortable talking with me considering their daughter's failing grade in my class. Quite the opposite was true. They expressed the confidence that she would prevail in the course later on.

In all, I exchanged names with about five or six people, although I do not remember any of their names. I must have been in some type of shock.

Comparing Cordiality

The church members I met were warm and friendly toward me. However, it would be fair to say that they were far more affectionate toward each other. Initially, I thought that this might be a racial thing. After reflecting on this, I decided that this difference in behavior could be explained by preexisting friendships. After all, these people had just met me.

Surprises

There were a few surprises. First, the service lasted an hour and forty-five minutes. We were on our feet for the first thirty minutes singing. The second surprise was that there is some type of "swap" program going on among

African American and Caucasian churches in July. Some people I met assumed that I was swapping churches that morning, but I did not correct them. Another surprise was that the head pastor of this church was going to be installed as a bishop the next week. There was some type of conference scheduled, and everyone was very excited about it. My favorite surprise occurred when the pastor was discussing the upcoming conference. He spent several minutes advising the congregation to wear black underwear if they chose to wear white clothes. This type of realistic advice would have never been tolerated in my childhood church. This congregation, however, enjoyed the humorous break and seemed a degree more connected to this pastor because of it.

FINDING MY FEET AT MY IN-LAWS'

One day, I had arrived home from work and my wife was very excited. Her father had called, and all the "men" in the family were being summoned. He was adding a room to their house and planned to complete the project over a weekend. Her parents live on a mountain in rural Pennsylvania, which is a friendly but country area where gender roles are more strictly observed. They have male rituals like hunting, playing poker, and building projects that I had never been exposed to. I told my wife that I had no construction-type skills and would just get in the way. My wonderful, new wife, however, explained that since I was new to the family, I should take this request very seriously. My rejection of this invitation could have been viewed as insulting.

The drive to my father-in-law's house took about four hours, and we arrived late Friday evening. Everyone was rousted up before sunrise. As I came down to breakfast and looked around, I immediately noticed my clothes were not right. They all had jeans like me but also had work shirts and work boots. The colors they wore were blue, brown, or gray. I wore a brightly colored Hawaiian shirt and sandals. My hair was not all that long, but it was longer than any of their "buzz cuts." The conversation at breakfast was lively and confusing. My relatives were speaking English but included words and references that I had never heard previously. In a room full of white people, I felt very much like a minority.

After breakfast, all the men were to be divided into teams. There were about fifteen guys, ranging from eighteen to sixty-five years of age. I felt like the kid who was always picked last. Eventually, my stepson and I were assigned what was considered a pretty easy job. We were to build struts for the roof. I remember that Uncle Sam gave us directions. He spoke quickly and referred to tools and procedures that were foreign to me. He started to get irritated with my questions, so I stopped asking them. My wife, a strong businesswoman, slipped back into her expected female role of cooking and "fetching" the men beverages as they worked. I remember being teased by the guys because my wife was concerned that I would cut off one or more fingers on the table saw.

The job took my stepson and me longer than was expected. I recall Uncle Sam calling down from the roof, "Those pieces had better be done by the time I need them." I was trying to fit in, but I could not get over the feeling of being uncomfortable in my own skin.

To make a long story short, the struts were completed, and I did not lose any fingers. I had never built anything before and was proud of my work. When it came time to put our struts in place, Uncle Sam went overboard with praise. My wife was called to witness my "fine struts." I know that their intentions were for me to feel good and accepted, but it had the opposite effect: I felt like they had very low expectations for me. Luckily, the adult in me was able to focus on what they had intended me to feel.

SOME REFLECTIONS

As I reflect about this essay and my experience at the church, I feel more empathetic to minority students' feelings. These children feel afraid, self-conscious, and out of place. These feelings, although in different degrees, would be the same for those who are only minorities while in my classroom.

There are several things that I could do to help my minority students before they even enter my room. I could plant the seeds of expected success by decorating the room with motivational posters involving minorities. I could do research on minority mathematicians and figure out a way to incorporate them into my curriculum. Listening to some popular hip-hop or rap music might help me understand their culture a bit more, and maybe I could find a way to use it in my class. I can go over my class roster with another teacher to ensure that I will be able to correctly pronounce their names. By having a clear list of rules and class procedures prepared before school starts, I will be prepared to create a safe environment for all my students.

In the beginning of the school year, the comfort of my students will be my first priority. I will greet my students at the door with a smile and a few kind words. There will be some lively music playing in the background as they enter.

The focus of the first day will be to share information about each other. During the first weeks, I will establish the classroom as my turf and teach my rules and procedures. I will make it clear that the rules and procedures are in place to create a safe learning environment for everyone. I will convince my students that I will do everything in my power to help them be successful. I will do my best to give the freshmen advice about navigating schooling, and I will make myself a resource for any type of questions they may have. I will encourage my students to join sports teams and get involved with the diverse school clubs that are available. Calling parents and telling them good things about their children would help create the taste for success.

I started off this essay whining about having to go to church for this assignment. I did not enjoy the assignment, but I did learn from it. Being a minority is far more complex than I had ever imagined. I may never fully understand why my diverse learners do some of the things they do, but I am willing to try. As I look at the previous paragraph, I realize that there is at least one of those things I could do right now. I am going to make it my mission to convince all my students that there are good reasons for them to go to college, and that seems like a good start.

15

Experiencing the Minority as the Only White in Church, the Only Woman in Corporate Meetings, and as a Denominational Minority

BETTY DANZI

I chose to attend a church service with a predominantly African American congregation (actually, I only saw one other nonblack person in the congregation, and she appeared to be part of an interracial couple). For me, the minority experience started in the parking lot. As I got out of my car to walk toward the church, I was very aware that I was the only white person in the crowded parking lot. When anyone made eye contact with me, I found myself smiling and saying good morning, but on the inside I was very nervous. In addition to being aware that I was different, I think a big part of my nervousness came from the feeling that I would be perceived as an outsider. I was afraid of being discovered as someone who was there to observe their worship (spy) rather than really participate in worship with them.

The greeter at the door welcomed me, shook my hand, and gave me a bulletin. As he took my hand, I worried that my hand felt cold and clammy. I was too nervous to say anything more than "Good morning." I entered the church, found a row of empty seats near the back, and walked to the far side where a family was already sitting. I asked if the seat next to them was open and received a curious look but was told that I could sit there. The row of seats on the other side of me quickly filled with the exception of the seat right next to me.

The choir sat at the back of the stage and was wearing purple and white robes. I remember thinking that I was glad I had chosen to wear a purple sweater that morning, as if in some way my clothing color choice helped me to fit in (silly). The music began and the music director led the singing. As we sang together, my nervousness subsided. Although I didn't know the songs, they were pleasant, worshipful, and not much different from the songs we sing at my own church. The main difference was that the music director was very animated and occasionally added a few dance steps to his singing.

The singing was interspersed with praying. Some members of the congregation participated in the prayer by responding with loud "Amens" and other comments. The singing and worship time lasted for about forty-five minutes. Most of this time was spent standing and singing, while many people clapped and swayed from side to side, with the occasional person adding a dance-type movement or a hand held up in the air. The socially acceptable levels of volume and movement were more than at my own church.

Next, the music director encouraged everyone to turn and greet their neighbors before sitting down. After having just shared a common worship experience, it was not intimidating to interact with those people closest to me. Everyone seemed happy to see each other, and many people were hugging. No one attempted to hug me, but everyone greeted me warmly and shook my hand. After we were seated, the last song began for the offertory. The ushers walked in with baskets and stood at certain places around the room. One at a time, each row of people walked to the front to place their offering into the basket. When I realized that I would have to stand up while others watched me walk to the basket, my self-consciousness about being white returned. I felt like all eyes were on me, wondering why I was there. In my church, we just pass the basket. Although I thought that walking the offering to the basket was a nice idea, I couldn't wait to retake my seat.

The pastor walked onto the stage to deliver his sermon. He began by inviting everyone to open their Bible and follow along while he read a passage of scripture. I had my Bible but found myself fumbling to find the correct scripture reference. I couldn't remember what verse he had just said to find. As we stood up, I was still turning pages, wondering if everyone around me noticed that I was slow in finding the passage. After the passage was read, we sat back down and the pastor began his sermon.

The pastor spoke in a conversational tone; he would stop and ask members of the congregation if they found what he said to be true in their own lives. People stood or called out at various times to acknowledge that the message was personal and meaningful to them. Having the congregation stand and respond while the pastor spoke was new for me and at times seemed distracting. A number of times during the message, the pastor became very loud and animated in making his point, and the congregation responded in kind, until almost everyone was standing or clapping. The pastor would then return to a normal speaking voice to continue with his sermon, and everyone would sit back down.

The end of the sermon was particularly emotional and very loud, with many people standing, dancing, or sobbing. At this time, I felt uncomfortable and unsure about what was coming next. I had no previous similar experience to tell me what to expect. This excitement continued for several minutes before the pastor began to pray. He led a prayer of confession and salvation followed by an altar call. After the altar call, the pastor made a few announcements about upcoming events and then dismissed everyone, saying, "I hope to see you back here for tonight's service." I wondered if this invitation included even me.

After the service ended, people seemed interested in either speaking with their friends, or exiting the church quickly. I couldn't see myself interrupting an ongoing conversation, so I joined the crowd that was exiting the church. In the parking lot, people were hugging and saying good-byes to one another. No one seemed to notice or care that I was there. I got to my car and was glad that come next Sunday, I would be back in my own familiar church.

Some Reflections

I think the experience helped me to see what it feels like to be an outsider. I hope that it will help me become more sensitive to the feelings of minorities and newcomers at both my school and church. From this experience, I can see that the worship style of any church (including my own church) is based on the accepted culture of the majority. In spite of my self-conscious feelings, I did enjoy the message and the time of worship. However, I probably won't choose to attend this church again unless invited by a friend.

THE ONLY WOMAN IN CORPORATE MEETINGS

There have been other times in my life when I felt like a minority. Years ago when I first entered the business world as a computer consultant, I found myself being the only woman in the room at many corporate meetings. It was hard enough to be young and feel the pressure to perform, but I also had the added pressure to prove that as a woman, I was at least as competent as my male peers. In many situations, I felt uncomfortable and excluded. One time, the partners of my firm (all men) held a bimonthly office meeting at an exclusive Washington, DC, club that did not permit female members (only good ol' boys). My employer had to make special arrangements to allow the female employees to enter the club in order to attend the meeting. It was a frustrating time!

After two years with this company, I saw less qualified men get promoted before me. When I spoke with a partner about the situation, I was told that "life is not fair" and I should deal with it. That day, I went to the ladies' room and cried. I was angry at myself for "acting emotional, like a woman" (but I made sure that no one else would see me in the ladies' room).

When traveling for business, I was often surprised that people in the northern and western states would say things like, "Until I worked with you, I thought all people from the South were supposed to be slow." It was difficult to walk into situations where I knew that, just because of my home state and accent (which actually is quite mild), people were going to negatively prejudge me. I remember spending a lot of energy getting myself mentally ready to meet each new client. It was exhausting.

By the time I left the firm, I had been promoted to the same level as or higher than my male colleagues. This achievement, however, took a lot of hard work. During this season of my life, I always felt that my performance had to be outstanding because, in a way, I represented all women in the workforce.

THE PROTESTANT IN A CATHOLIC ENVIRONMENT

Another time I felt like a minority was when I first attended the Catholic Church with my husband-to-be. Although I had grown up in a (Protestant) church, I quickly found out that I knew nothing about what to do or when to do it in the Catholic Mass. It wasn't obvious from my skin color or gender that I didn't fit in, but it was very obvious by my awkward actions. I didn't know when to kneel, when to stand, when or what to respond to, in unison, with the congregation, including when and how to make the sign of the cross. Because I wasn't Catholic, I couldn't even take part in communion.

After going to Catholic Mass several times, things became more familiar, and within a couple of months, I almost "looked" like I fit in. However, each week during communion, I was left sitting alone in the pew, as an uncomfortable reminder that I still didn't really belong. Even now, after twenty years of attending Catholic Masses for various family occasions (weddings, funerals, etc.), I still feel like an outsider because I never chose to convert.

I feel like the non-Catholic girl in the extended family. Even though we were married in the Baptist church, we also went through premarriage counseling with a priest and had our marriage blessed as a sacrament in the Catholic Church. However, some members of my husband's extended family never accepted our marriage because I am not Catholic. These family members have treated me as an outsider for over twenty years. However, I am quite sure that they are not even aware of the hurtful things they say and the impact that these comments have on me. At his family functions, Catholic values and traditions are elevated (since they are the "dominant cultural group"), and my values and traditions are devalued and marginalized. For me, it is an uncomfortable situation.

TEACHING IMPLICATIONS

I know from my own "minority" experiences that it is hard to want to participate if you don't feel like you fit in. Just as I felt uncomfortable and wanted to sit in the back (unnoticed) when I visited an all-black church, I think that many minority students feel like they do not fit in with what is being taught in this classroom.

There may be several changes that would be worth trying in order to reach these students. Perhaps it would help to hang up posters in the classroom of cultural heroes or show video clips of cultural heroes—for example, the video clip of a black male art director discussing how important it is to have accurate area measurements when he designs a movie set (http://www.thefutureschannel.com/dockets/hands-on_math/the_art_director/).

As a math teacher, every time a new math concept is introduced, I will try to relate how this concept is useful in the real world. I also think that discussing the rich history of how mathematics has evolved and the contributions made by various world cultures is an important way to help students connect with the subject. I also like the idea of profiling biographies of great minority mathematicians and their contributions to the field (e.g., http://www.math.buffalo.edu/mad/madgreatest.html#masters). The more I help students connect with what I'm teaching, the more likely they will be motivated to learn. My own experiences as a minority have helped me to better empathize with my minority students and motivate me to strive to create a more meaningful educational experience for them.

16

Experiencing the Minority at a Black Church, Fitting in as a Reverse Minority in School, *and* Thinking Religion "Outside the Box"

BRIAN BONGIOVANNI

While there is certainly no way for members of the majority group to truly experience the thoughts and feelings of minorities, those feelings and thoughts may be approximated by putting themselves in a situations where they are the minority. In this vein, I, a Caucasian teacher in a predominantly African American school, attended a predominantly African American church in hopes of seeing through the lenses of my students. I think that this experience resembles that of my at-risk students, because I find no value in organized religion, much as some my students appear to find no relevant value in school for their lives, for different reasons. After reflecting on this experience, I gained some insight into my students' lives and will adjust my teaching strategies to better address their needs.

Cultural Elements

My church experience opened my eyes to some cultural elements of the African American community. The first element that I observed was the style and formalness of attire. I visited a church in a low socioeconomic neighborhood, yet the clothes that the congregation wore appeared expensive. I also observed that the entire congregation was dressed very formally, truly living up to the notion of "Sunday clothes." Having observed white congregations as well, whose dress runs the gambit from golf shirts and slacks to suits and ties, I was relieved to have worn a suit; had I worn anything less, I would have felt that, in some way, I had disrespected this church's community.

The next cultural element I observed was a sense of family. This sense of family extended into the parking lot. Greetings were loud, boisterous, and friendly. Greetings sometimes led to stories that ended in laughter. Inside the church, people reached across pews to shake hands or hug. While everyone was dressed very formally, the atmosphere before the service was substantially less formal and very relaxed.

The service I observed was much less structured than other services I have observed. The congregation, the choir, the deacons, and the preacher all seemed like one entity for the church. Sometimes the preacher's words would just lead into a song by the choir, something that never happened in other churches I have observed. The preacher and the choir got constant verbal and physical affirmations from the congregation during the service. The choir and the congregation often swayed together and clapped during hymns. Most members seemed very engaged in service.

The final cultural element that I observed was that the preacher was very passionate and showered the congregation with his passion during his sermon. In most white churches I have observed, the preacher often seems like he is disseminating information that he has learned and passing enlightenment on to his congregation. The preacher I observed for this experience seemed to be trying to inspire rather than to teach. His volume rose and fell to emphasize certain points and the climaxes of his stories. He used his arms and hands to point at the congregation, appeal to God, and create a barrier against the devil and his works. He was very entertaining and commanded the attention of his congregation. He was indisputably the leader of his church.

Experiencing the Minority

Being the minority in the room actually started for me in the parking lot. As I stated earlier, this congregation's sense of family began outside, and I was obviously a newcomer. I tried my best to observe them but tried to avoid extended eye contact. However, when I made eye contact with anyone, I addressed them with "Good Morning." I read a story once about a runner who traveled a lot. He said that when running in places he didn't know across the world, no matter how hostile or uncomfortable the areas he ran into were, if he initiated verbal contact by saying, "Hello" or "Good morning" with a big smile, the majority would respond in kind. I have taken that to heart since reading it. I was new to this situation; therefore, I should make the effort to communicate. The members of the congregation whom I greeted unanimously responded in kind, although not with the handshakes or sense of family they greeted other congregation members.

Once inside the church, the sense of being an outsider became overwhelming. Since the church was full, I had to sit close to others. Therefore, their sense of family was all the more obvious to me, and I became entirely self-conscious. Everyone around me seemed to have a history of shared experiences and stories that bonded them together. Lacking this history and feeling like an intruder, I wished for this experience to go by quickly. Observing African American culture for a class, in the setting of organized religion, for which I find no value, seemed like a betrayal of something that the members of the congregation held very dear. I wished I could say I was sorry.

Seeking to Connect

I was unsuccessful in engaging members of the congregation except for one family. Most of the congregants I greeted were very cordial in response, but that is where the engagement ended. We had no immediately obvious shared interests, and they had no motivation to prolong the conversation. The one family that I was successful in talking to had a baby. Since I have a five-month-old and a two-year-old, we could share stories about a common interest. I showed them pictures of my children and they showed off theirs. It is amazing how our two families are from two very different cultures, but baby stories are remarkably similar, if not identical. Possibly, if the whole world could reflect on that phenomenon, the United States would have a little less cultural tension.

A Surprise

My biggest surprise was the behavior of the children and young adults in the congregation. As previously stated, I visited a church service in a lower socioeconomic area that was predominantly African American. Based on some preconceived notions of behavior problems in public schools, one would assume that the children would misbehave and be disruptive. Yet, there were almost no obvious disruptions, and smaller disruptions were often corrected with nonverbal redirection. The children seemed engaged and, at the very least, continually respectful of the environment of the church. While this was surprising, after observing the physical movement during the service, singing, church-community interaction, and correlating that information into reading Hutchison's *Teaching Diverse Learners*, it seems obvious that to have successful minority students, the school system needs to be modified.

FITTING IN AS A REVERSE MINORITY IN SCHOOL

I can recall two other relevant experiences where I was clearly the "minority." The first experience was when my family moved from a predominantly white school in Wooster, Ohio, to a predominantly black school in Laurinburg, North Carolina. When I initially visited the school, I was terrified that I would be the only white student enrolled. Fortunately, I was not the only white student, but I was certainly the minority, being white, in my middle school. I remember one incident very vividly: I was in band class standing in the back of a steaming hot trailer with the rest of the drum section. I wanted very badly to play the drums because my father had played them as a student. There were seven of us: two white students, including me, and five black students. During one of the breaks, one of the black students looked over at me and said, "God damn, you have a lot of hair on your arms." I guess since I was Italian and the hair was jet black, it really stood out to him. He had no obvious hair on his arms, and neither did the rest of the black students. He started telling all the other drummers to look at my arms, pointing out how hairy they were.

Up until that point in life, I had never been consciously aware of the hair on my arms. Certainly, as a member of the drum section, I could not hide my arms. I became intensely self-conscious and uncomfortable. The other students began to laugh, and I could feel myself turning red and beginning to tear up, which made the other students pick on me that much more. I wanted to quit the band more than anything in the world. Unfortunately, my parents would not hear of their son quitting anything once he started. I dreaded band class each day for weeks but knew I had to attend even if it meant being ridiculed.

After those weeks of trying to disappear and failing, I began trying to fit in. I don't know if it was conscious or not, but I began listening to rap music because that is what the other drum students were listening to at the time. I memorized lyrics and beats, much to my parents' displeasure. I used this to gain enough "respect," such that even the student who had first called me out and I became friends. We both became members of the pep band. He played the snare drum, and I played the bass drum. I became one of the few students who could flip back and forth between cultures.

I believe that the consequence of this experience is that I became aware of racial differences and my own racial identity. Janet Helms (1984) discusses stages of *white identity development*. The first stage is *contact*. I knew that black students had different-colored skin, but I did not realize that black students noticed the differences in white children. By coming into contact with blacks, and listening to rap music and learning the beats to fit in with my black classmates, I passed through *disintegration* by overly identifying with black culture. By beginning to understand my own racial identity in my early middle school years I was able to reach the stage of *autonomy* soon after high school. By this time, I was able to intellectually and emotionally accept racial differences and was fairly cross-culturally proficient. While the move to Laurinburg was a difficult time and an awkward adjustment for me, I think that being thrust into a situation where I was the minority eventually molded me into a more open-minded human being with the ability to understand the concept of diversity.

THINKING RELIGION "OUTSIDE THE BOX"

The second relevant experience I have in being the minority is in the religious context. My father was Catholic but converted to Methodist after he got married. My parents are religious and demanded that we attend Sunday school, church services, and youth group all through my school years. From as early as I can remember, I believed in God but felt complete disdain for organized religion. I remember going to many different types of churches before being confirmed, as part of our confirmation classes. While attending these classes, I saw the many different ways people worshipped their "gods": each one different, and each one thought they were worshipping the "right" way. As I grew older and became more educated, I began to wonder why these religions were any different than the ancient religions of the Africans, South Americans, or Native Americans.

This is a relevant "minority" experience because a majority of people would rather that one belongs to any organized religion—even if it is not theirs—than no religion at all. Since I do not find value in organized religion, my opinion on issues such as God, the afterlife, and the way to lead a good life are often discounted because they are not "doctrine" or standard. I used to experience frustration when grappling with this issue, but I have now come to accept that since my beliefs are not aligned with the cultural norms, they will mostly be ignored.

The consequence of this ongoing minority experience is a feeling of empathy for students who do not value a traditional school education. I can sense the frustration of artists, musicians, writers, and students who are not necessarily academically gifted but good with repairing cars or building things with their hands. Their needs are ignored by a school system that only pushes and values students who want to pursue a college education. While more and more vocational and arts schools are phased out of public funding, students with those aptitudes will tune out of classes and turn inside themselves much as I do during any religious discussions. The difference is that I have the option to avoid my frustration, whereas they are forced day after day to take part in seemingly meaningless activities in school.

School Connections: Breaking the Self-Fulfilling Prophecy

Teaching at a school where the student population is 98 percent African American and mostly at risk makes identifying the minority experience of students difficult. When new students first come to our school, they feel that they are in the "bad" school because they are "bad" students. A majority of our students find it hard to believe that we do not view them in the same light they have be conditioned to view themselves. Breaking this self-fulfilling prophecy takes time and patience, but most of the students begin to make an effort by the middle of the year. Since we are now retaining more students year to year, that process is speeding up because we have cultural capital or acceptable social conventions with returning students who help the new students.

In one of my classes, there was one student who really exhibited what I understand to be the *minority effect.* He was rumored to have been in a gang. He ran his household. He was either completely silent and withdrawn, or disruptive and violent. He spent at least one-third of the year suspended out of school. He had one friend in the school and did not care for the other students. Every effort made to reach out to him was rejected. Yet, the occasional work that he completed was of high quality and possessed thoughtful responses.

One Monday, about a month before the end of school, we were doing an assignment—and he was refusing to do work. When students refuse to do any work, I place paper and a pencil on their desk, and let them know it is there in case they change their mind. I have found this strategy much more effective than threats, detention, or yelling. As I circulated through the room, I encouraged this student to make an effort. He pushed his paper and pencil on the floor and told me to go away and that he wasn't doing it. Since he was disrespectful in front of the whole class, I asked him to step outside and "Take five" (i.e., reflect on his behavior for five minutes) to get himself together.

Once outside he said, "You don't run me." I have heard this from students before, but not quite with the hostility with which he spoke. I assured him that I was not trying to "run him." He thought I was mocking him, so he came toward me aggressively and issued a challenge to a fight. I turned sideways and let him know that was a bad choice and that I would be back in a couple of minutes when he "cooled down." When I came back to get him, he returned to his seat but did not attempt any of the class's assignment.

After reflecting on the incident, I wondered if his anger toward me was because I was white. While he had confronted other students, he had never confronted other staff. I am not sure of the reason for this. Possibly, it was because I continue to push him to do his work, even if he remains quiet while not doing work. Possibly, he associates white men with authority over which he has no control. Since he never opened up to me, I cannot be sure. The incident never presented itself again, but his underachievement remained. Based on my classroom observations, it appeared that academic work represented no value in his life; he probably saw the streets as his only way to survive in life. My reflection of this experience is that I and the system failed this student. I need to work harder to better understand and help these students who are otherwise capable but are not motivated to work.

TEACHING IMPLICATIONS

My minority experience highlighted the way that lack of cultural capital can hold someone back in social interactions. Not only was I visibly different by the color of my skin, but I was unable to bridge that gap due to my lack of shared experiences and history. Only the shared experience of raising children allowed me to engage one family. That reinforces to me that teachers must reach out to minority students in order to bridge the cultural gap between the student and the rest of the class.

Teachers in low-income schools with high diversity must teach with agency to be effective (Hutchison, unpublished manuscript). That is, they need to help students to become self-motivated. I would define teaching with agency as a situation whereby teachers understand themselves, are sensitive and flexible to the diverse needs of their students, and create a community atmosphere within their classroom so that all students can learn because their needs are met. There are many ways to teach with agency. Just from observing a church service, I know that I will need to incorporate more movement and allow more freedom of responses and freedom in discussions. Taking the time to understand cultural norms is another way to teach with agency. The culture of the classroom should recognize the diverse culture of the students, not just the middle-class policy makers and teachers.

17

Surviving in Church, *and* Understanding the Minority through Interracial Marriage

CRYSTAL SISK

What does "experiencing the minority" mean? Is it simply socializing with people who differ from you in terms of race, religion, or sexual orientation? No, it means putting yourself in an environment in which you are the minority. For me as a white woman, it meant attending a predominantly African American church. It was important for me, a future educator, to have a better understanding of the emotions and experiences that minority students are forced to face in the public school system. In hopes of gaining insight into minority students' world, I attended church service at Fresh Start Church.

Intimidated

From the moment I pulled into the parking lot of Fresh Start Church, my heart started racing. I immediately began drawing the attention of the people arriving for their usual Sunday service. There were many people who offered me a warm smile and a quick hello as I proceeded into the church. Yet, I couldn't help but notice that some were not enthusiastic of me being in their "territory." I saw a group of women roll their eyes as I passed by them in the parking lot. Many of the churchgoers were whispering and obviously attempting to figure out why I was at their church on Sunday morning instead of my own. I won't lie; I was extremely intimidated, although I had no real reason to feel that way. You see, I am a white woman married to a black man. I am used to being part of a minority group in society even though I am a member of the majority race. I have attended black family reunions where I was obviously in the minority. Perhaps, the presence of my husband at the reunions had given me a feeling of security that I lacked walking in alone to a "foreign" church.

Watching the Joy of Others

I had decided from the beginning to sit in the back of the chapel. As I walked through the church doors, I was immediately greeted by the minister and his wife. They were very warm and welcoming. They proceeded to introduce me to other people standing nearby. It was very loud in the entry area. The room was filled with sounds of laughter and nonstop talking. I continued to get both curious looks and disdainful glances. Interestingly, my first reaction was to look around the room and try to find another white person. I initiated very few conversations and restricted myself to repetitive phrases such as "Hello" and "Good morning." I lacked the confidence to do much more. I just wanted to find a seat. As I looked around, it was amazing to watch the congregation as they greeted one another. People seemed to be intimate with the details of each other's lives. They hugged and slapped each other on the back.

Watching the people walk into the chapel was quite an experience. Everyone was dressed in their "Sunday best." The men were wearing suits and ties. All the women wore dresses and beautiful jewelry. This contrasted greatly with the "white" churches I had attended in the past. People wore jeans and were dressed very casually. There were a long list of announcements and prayer lists before the service actually begin. The sermon was much more dynamic than most I had heard from white ministers. The language was in some ways simpler and less "preachy." The whole process seemed to not be as rigid as compared to white churches. The music sung by the choir was not as somber and was much louder. People weren't just rising and taking their hymnals out and quietly singing along. At Fresh Start Church, the congregation was loud and expressive. People were dancing and raising their arms in the air. In many ways, I felt jealous of their experiences. They were obviously at "home." I felt awkward trying to sing along and keep the rhythm of the beats.

The service lasted longer than any church service I had ever attended. Perhaps it was a long service because I felt like an outsider the whole time. This was in spite of the fact that no one had said anything directly to me pointing out that I didn't belong there.

UNDERSTANDING THE MINORITY THROUGH INTERRACIAL MARRIAGE

I have often felt like a minority in society. I am in an interracial marriage: I am white and my husband is black. There have been many occasions when I have been the only white person at my husband's family gatherings or part of the only interracial couple at a resort or restaurant. It has taken me many years to fully adjust to being a minority at certain times and places. It has been an eye-opening experience for me to realize how often I have benefited unconsciously from "white privilege."

In terms of being a minority at my husband's family gatherings, it was very scary and overwhelming at first. My initial reaction was to be shy. I stayed glued to my husband's side. I did not go out of my way to initiate conversations or join in on debates, jokes, or group activities that were taking place. I was petrified. I was usually a confident person who loved to join in on a good debate. I always had plenty I wanted to say, but at these meetings, I was too scared to even open my mouth. I felt like an outsider. I began to dread having to participate in family gatherings. It began to create tension between my husband's family and me. They began to say that I thought I was better than them. They said I was a snob. Of course, that wasn't the case. I was simply just a minority who felt out of place.

In the end, certain family members began to go out of their way to include me in "family life." I began to feel more comfortable and willing to participate in conversations and so forth. Eventually, people who had considered me a snob began to apologize to me for assuming that my shyness meant that I had an "attitude."

I no longer feel like an outsider at family gatherings even though I am still the minority. I have learned that the actions and preconceived notions of both the majority and the minority often create unnecessary conflict.

REFLECTIONS AND TEACHING IMPLICATIONS

My experiences in life and participation in the Experiencing the Minority project have greatly influenced the way I perceive the issues facing diverse learners. I clearly understand the importance of taking a moment to step back and consider the motives behind students' actions in the classroom. It is often too easy for teachers to make broad assumptions and label students based on "frames of mind" (Hutchison, unpublished manuscript, 164). Students are falling through the cracks because no one has taken the time to understand their behavior. They are victims of stereotype threat.

When I felt like an outsider, I distanced myself from other people. I became reserved and unwilling to share my thoughts and feelings. I was labeled a "snob" who thought she was better than others. Diverse learners experience the same fears and anxieties. Students who are minorities in schools struggle to be included in the classroom community. Diverse learners are often treated as outsiders by their peers as well as educators. Educators must teach with agency (Hutchison, unpublished manuscript, 141). In this respect, I want to be a teacher whose philosophy is like that of the "tutor." Linda Winfield described tutors as "teachers who took personal responsibility for helping their struggling students to improve. They provided them the tutelage they needed to become achievers" (Winfield, 1986, as cited in Hutchison, unpublished manuscript, 149). Teachers need to create a sense of autonomy in their students (Hutchison, unpublished manuscript, 141). We must take the time to accommodate the special needs of diverse learners, based on the understanding that the cultural rules that students live by outside the classroom are not always compatible with classroom polices. The teacher sets the tone for the whole classroom. Beginning on the first day of class, educators must begin creating an environment where every child feels safe to be themselves and respected. At times, it may be beneficial for the teacher to point out his or her differences or even flaws. We must look at each student as an individual with feelings, motivations, and a desire to achieve.

If I could change the public school system's approach to diverse learners, the first thing I would call for is more education for teachers. Often, teachers who fail to address the needs of minority students do so because they lack training. In most cases, a white suburban teacher has no clue about the struggles that face his or her minority students outside the classroom. She or he cannot see how a black student's rough and tough facade is a necessary tool for survival in their neighborhood. Policies and standards in the classroom need to be fluid. Teachers need to be able to see the whole child and adjust to meet students' needs.

Inside Fresh Start Church in Matthews, I became the minority or the "other." I sat in the church feeling scared, overwhelmed, and out of place. My personality changed, and I became unusually reserved. Diverse learners experience similar emotions every single day in the classroom. It is up to the educator to create a new reality for these students. The student in the back of the classroom who doesn't participate in class and seems to have a discipline problem may just be a scared child feeling out of place in a sea of strangers.

18

Differences on a Common Ground, *and* the Only Guy at an All-Girls Party

DAVID W. CORNETT

In the school setting, teachers encounter many different types of diversity. America's schools are a melting pot for a myriad of cultures and races, which is a good thing, but it may prove to be a challenge for the teachers if the classroom is of a race or culture other than their own. This challenge is usually encountered for the first time in the classroom and must be prepared for, if possible. One good way teachers can prepare for situations where they either are the minority or have minority students is for them to put themselves in the situation ahead of time.

For my Experiencing the Minority project, I visited a church back in my hometown called Angel Baptist Church. This church is predominantly African American and presented a fantastic opportunity for me to gain that feeling of being a minority. The church is very small, with about seventy-five members, none of whom I had met before, which made me very nervous. I knew I should expect to feel a little bit awkward in this church, but I felt comforted by the fact that the church group and I had something in common: we were both Christians and Baptists. I felt going into this church was less threatening because it was easier to find some common ground on which to build a foundation and establish connections with a different group of people.

The first steps I took through that door were the scariest I had ever taken, but I soon found many similarities between their church setting and mine. I sat in the back, so as not to draw too much attention to myself, but it turned out I drew a lot of attention anyway, since I was the only white person in the congregation. The entire worship experience was pleasant but very different than what I was used to. Their way of worshiping God was very different in that they were much more mobile and vociferous during their worship. The African American culture has always been seen to include passionate responses to praising God, and this church was no exception. During every song (there was about an hour of singing), I saw hands flying up in the air and people moving about while many "Amens" and "Hallelujahs" rang through the air. The preaching was also very different in that the pastor became progressively more excited and louder than I have ever seen before, along with about three testimonials from various members of the congregation. It was very strange comparing and contrasting my church experience here with the ones I have had before, because even though we are of the same religion *and* denomination, their culture made the service profoundly different.

After the service and preaching, I felt more the minority than ever. It was a little scary because I pictured everyone around me judging me and questioning my motives for being there, even though this was only the case with a few of the members. Every once in a while I would get a glance of some elderly woman or a curious child peeping over the pews, but overall the group seemed very welcoming. There was a break between the singing and the preaching, where everyone got up and shook hands with one another. Many people just seemed to avoid me in my spot and conversed with their friends and family. I half-expected this since I was new and a minority in their group, but it was still disconcerting for I felt I should be welcomed even more for being new and different from everyone else.

One Connection and Its Consequence

While the congregants laughed and talked with one another, I remained standing in my pew, but soon quite a few people came over telling me how glad they were that I came, and some encouraged me to come back, which made me feel a little better about being there, but not better about being the only noticeable minority—an awareness that largely isolated me from enjoying the same experience as the people around me were having. I was able to actually talk to quite a few people this way and found out I had graduated high school with one lady's son. This little break was nice for it helped me to become more comfortable with everyone else and encouraged me talk to and connect with a small but good-sized number of the people at the church that day. This was a good surprise, for I had expected to just go to the church, sit in the back, and leave, but once they began talking to me, I found it much easier to converse and have a good time while I was there.

THE ONLY GUY AT AN ALL-GIRLS PARTY

My friend Mary is a member of a sorority. One day, she invited me to her birthday dinner. She said that it was only going to be a few people and that it wouldn't be awkward for me in any way. Well, when I entered the Olive Garden, I discovered three tables arranged lengthwise with about thirty girls sitting there. To make matters worse, the only available seat was at the direct opposite of my friend, and I had no idea who any of these other people were! At first, I was very angry and upset with Mary for bringing me to a place where I didn't know anyone and was the only guy. I sat at the end and tried to make conversation with the girls around me, to no avail. All of them only seemed interested in talking with those they were comfortable with, so they paid me no attention and basically pretended that I wasn't there. With no one to talk to, I felt miserable and lonely. I was the minority: a guy in a sea of girls, and I had no hope for a good evening, for I constantly projected what these girls must be thinking about me and was nauseated by how miserable I was in this situation.

Throughout the dinner, I just sat in my seat and listened to these girls' conversations and tried to put in my own opinion about what they were talking about, which made the conversation even more awkward and strange, for they felt I was listening in on their private conversation. I was bored and had nothing to do, so I sat there in silence for the majority of the dinner and ended up leaving much earlier than everyone else without even saying good-bye to my friend because I didn't feel like embarrassing myself by interrupting her discussion with her friends.

What the Girls Thought about Me

The next day, Mary came up to me and asked me why I looked so miserable at the dinner. She relayed to me what everyone thought of me, using adjectives like *shy* and *rude*, which was a complete misconception of what I actually am. I acted shy because I had no one to talk to, for I had met these girls on the spot, and from my personal point of view, it would have been rude to intrude in their conversations or "crash" a party that was not meant for me to attend.

SOME REFLECTIONS

In both of these experiences, I got a taste of being a minority student, although these were rare occasions in my life. I have always been comfortable in most settings because these are ones where I have always been in the majority or at least had one or two others with whom I could associate. In my experiences at Angel Baptist Church and Olive Garden, I did not have that little bit of comfort that usually meant a person of the same race or gender as me. If I felt this way as a more mature person, it is hard for me to imagine what it must be like for a child, whose mind is still in the developing process. Children are much more impressionable than adults. They do their best to take everything they sense around them, analyze it, and try to understand it based on their maturity level. Being a minority, however, is something that is very difficult to understand.

Race can be a huge issue for small children, since they tend to see each other as human equals and rarely view one another on the basis of skin color or gender until they get older. This may explain why boys and girls at a young age are always seen playing with one another, while boys and girls at an older age only play with others of the same sex. We tend to associate ourselves with people who share similar characteristics, but what if these characteristics cannot be found in anyone around us? This is the question that many minority students in American schools face every day. As young people, minority students may not understand their situations fully. They know they are different, but they cannot understand why, and this may lead to increased shyness and awkwardness in the classroom. This could possibly damage their self-esteem as they grow older. They will essentially isolate themselves because they realize they do not fit in, and without counseling, this could even lead to some kind of depression.

Teaching Implications

Based on my experiences, I believe that the teacher's duty is to keep children from feeling unwelcomed or isolated in the classroom. Students should be made to feel welcome, not necessarily in a conscious manner, but rather in a way that makes them know that they are included and are welcome. This is what many of the people at the Angel Baptist Church tried to do for me. One may argue that lonely students are at risk, so they must be engaged just as much, if not more, than the rest of the children in the classroom. Many teachers may try to avoid calling attention to minority students for fear of embarrassing them, but in reality this may instead hurt the students, for they are being neglected.

In my classroom, the minority children would be fully incorporated into the classroom discussions and actively partnered with their peers to make them feel comfortable talking, and eventually connecting, with the rest of the children in the room. This will also lead to friendships being formed with the hope of their full incorporation in out-of-school activities with the other children. Involvement is key to the success of the minority student, because being passive and leaving them alone will cause them to never come out of their proverbial shells.

I believe that many public school teachers in America do not know how to deal with minority students, since it is a new field for which they are not trained. Based on my minority experience activity, minority students can present a challenge to teachers especially in schools where this type of student is rare. In such cases, the teacher may just neglect them if they are not comfortable with addressing minority issues. Many teachers, I believe, should be introduced to teaching minority students in the whole classroom and must be taught the psychology of these students in the classroom and public school settings.

CONCLUSION

Experiencing the minority was a very hard thing for me to do. I finally got to understand what minority students experience every day in classrooms and how it must affect their schoolwork, their development, and their lives. Teachers must learn to become the keystones to teaching and working with this specific type of learner and must understand that if minority students are left feeling alone and abandoned, it can affect their future lives. Therefore, it is important to seek ways to help these students.

19

A White Female in the Class on the African Experience, North-South Linguistic Dichotomy, *and* Thinking about Marcus

WINFREE BRISLEY

Through a course I am taking at a university, I have had the unique experience, as a white person, of being a minority in the classroom. Because it is an actual classroom experience, it has given me real insight into how my students might feel as minorities in my future classes. In this class, I am one of only two white students, and the rest of the thirty or so members of the class are African American. In addition, the professor is African American, and the course is called "The Black Experience." Thus, not only am I a minority among my classmates and professor, but the content of the class is unfamiliar to me as well and does not relate to my cultural heritage.

I have noticed several aspects of the African American culture in my class. First, the professor does not lecture in a relatively even tone of voice for the entire class. In fact, sometimes, at moments that seem very random and unpredictable to me, he will suddenly say a word or phrase much more loudly than he was previously speaking. At first, this actually startled me because I was not expecting it. I think I may have even physically jumped a little in my seat the first time that he did this. This seems very similar to the way in which an African American preacher might use the volume of his or her voice to emphasize certain ideas.

Another aspect that I have noticed among my classmates and professor is a tendency toward movement. When I think back to classes taught by white professors, I remember many of them standing behind a podium for the entire length of the class as they delivered their lecture. However, my professor for this class tends to move quite a bit during his lecture. His movements are often subtle, taking a few steps in one direction or the other, or even swaying in his place. However, he never ends his lecture in the same place where he began it. Sometimes he will also make more obvious movements with his arms and hands when he is trying to emphasize a point. I have also noticed a tendency of my classmates to get up during the class and move around. I am not sure what they are actually doing, of course, but I have simply noticed more activity in this class than in others I have taken.

Being a minority in the classroom has been an unfamiliar and at times uncomfortable feeling for me. I remember vividly the first day of class. As I watched students file in and take their seats, I began to realize that the class was filling up and I was the only white student. This made me fairly uncomfortable, and I remember hoping every time I heard the door open that another white student would enter so that I would not feel so alone and out of place. By the time class began, I think there were about three other white students present, but it seems that two of them must have dropped the course because only one other white student remains at this late point in the semester.

Making Progress

I was able to move beyond my initial discomfort and actually began to appreciate the situation. I realized that it would be helpful for me in understanding what it feels like to be a minority. However, taking this mental approach did not alleviate all of my feelings of discomfort. For the first few weeks of class, I still had the distinct feeling that the professor was staring at me. As he lectured, he would often look in my direction and make eye contact with me, and I began to feel that he was looking at me more than he did other students. Eventually, I got over this feeling and realized that there are at least two possible explanations for this. One explanation is that I was oversensitive to his glances because I felt uncomfortable being a minority. The other is that

I tended to look up at him more than the other students so his eyes may have naturally been drawn in my direction.

For the first several weeks of class, I mostly kept to myself. I came into class, sat quietly before the lecture began, and then left immediately after it was over. No one attempted to communicate with me, and I did not attempt to communicate with them. However, before class one day, a male African American student approached me and asked what he had missed the previous class. I shared my notes with him, and we had a nice conversation. He was very cordial, and the fact that he approached me made me feel more comfortable in the class. Since then, I have initiated conversations with a couple of my classmates. In general, our exchanges have been brief and mostly consisted of the person answering the question I asked them, but they have certainly been cordial. It does seem that my classmates interact more with one another than with me or the other white student in the class. However, I would actually attribute this to the fact that many of the students seemed to already know one another prior to the class. Therefore, I do not think that they are actively excluding me.

NORTH–SOUTH LINGUISTIC DICHOTOMY

Several years ago, my husband and I moved to a suburb of Philadelphia for his job. It quickly became apparent to me that there are real differences between the northern part of the United States and the southern part, not the least of which is the accent. In addition to differences in accent, there were many differences in vocabulary that I noticed between southern and northern English. Though we were speaking the same language, there were times when I had no idea what people were talking about, due to the combination of accent and different vocabulary.

While in the North, I took a job as an instructional aide in a local elementary school, and my experiences there confirmed that I was certainly a minority when it came culture and, in particular, language. Though I cannot hear my southern accent, from the first word I spoke at this school, it became apparent to me that everyone else certainly heard my accent. In the beginning, I received constant comments on my accent. Some people seemed to find it endearing, but for other people, I was not so sure. Perhaps I was oversensitive, but I wondered if some people had the stereotype that southerners not only speak slowly but are intellectually slow.

Enduring My Accent-Related Issues

While my colleagues certainly noticed my accent and made comments about it, the students' reactions were much worse. Students told me that I talked "funny" or sounded "weird," and many wanted to know where I was from. I even occasionally heard some trying to imitate me. This made me self-conscious, and I felt that the students were sometimes making fun of my accent.

I became especially self-conscious about my accent in the cafeteria. The instructional aides at our school took turns monitoring the cafeteria in groups of two or three, and we were responsible for using a microphone to give students a two-minute warning and then later get them lined up for recess. At first, I did not mind making the announcements on the microphone. However, I soon realized that when I did, it seemed to encourage student commentary on my accent. For a while, I tried to avoid making announcements. When I could not avoid speaking on the microphone, I was extremely self-conscious and sometimes stumbled over my words. I knew that there was no reason to be embarrassed about my accent, but sometimes I could not help feeling out of place.

While my accent made me self-conscious among students, vocabulary and other cultural differences made me self-conscious around my adult colleagues. I ate lunch every day with the four third grade teachers with whom I worked. In our conversations, I was sometimes lost because I did not recognize a key word that they were using or did not understand some sort of cultural practice or phenomenon that they were discussing. Sometimes this caused me to withdraw from the conversation so that I would not have to ask them to explain things for me. Other times, I made comments that probably did not make sense because I did not really understand the topic of conversation. More often than not, I chose to remain quiet and not engage in the conversation. As I got to know them better, I realized that there was no reason for me to be embarrassed about asking for explanations, and I became less self-conscious and more involved.

THINKING ABOUT MARCUS

While I felt like a cultural minority in this school, I worked with a student who was a racial/ethnic minority, and he certainly exhibited the "minority experience" both inside and outside of the classroom. Marcus was a third grade African American student in whom I took a special interest during my time as an elementary aide. If I remember correctly, he was the only nonwhite student in his class and one of only about five nonwhite students in the whole third grade. However, he was not the only African American in his classroom because his teacher was African American. The racial dynamics of the third grade were fairly representative of the school as a whole. The school was located in a wealthy white neighborhood, and consequently the large majority of the students were white. However, a group of students lived in a nearby trailer park, and most of the minority students in the school, including Marcus, came from this area.

Classroom Struggles

I noticed Marcus early on in the school year because he tended to be in trouble. He often either acted out or did not do his work. In class, he tended to slump down in his seat and rarely seemed to be paying attention. He rarely stayed on task, and consequently, his work was often left incomplete. Because of this, Marcus's teacher often had me work one-on-one with him to help him complete his assignments. When we worked together, I found that he had very little self-confidence. Sometimes, I got the impression that he did not even want to attempt the assignments because he had already assumed that he would not be successful. I had to prod him every step of the way and assure him that he could, in fact, do the work.

On one particular occasion, Marcus and I were working on an assignment on a computer, in the back of the classroom. He was unsure about how to complete part of the assignment, and so I tried to ask him questions to help him figure it out rather than directly telling him the answer. It was not unusual for me to use this sort of strategy, and normally it worked fairly well. However, on this day, I think his frustrations hit the breaking point, and he blurted out something like, "I can't do this! I'm not like the other kids!" When I asked him why he thought he was different from the other students, he answered that it was because they were white. Marcus had come to associate being white with being smart and successful in school. Because he realized that he was racially different, he thought that he could not perform as well as they could in the classroom. I tried to assure Marcus that he was just as capable as the white students, but I am not sure that he was convinced. Being in a classroom where he was the only nonwhite student had clearly weighed down on Marcus, and his learning experiences suffered as a consequence.

Luckily for Marcus, his teacher realized what was going on with him in the classroom. She was well aware that he was falling behind and told me that she was determined to make sure that he was successful. I think she felt a special responsibility for Marcus because of their shared ethnic heritage. She began keeping him several days a week during lunch or recess time so that she could work with him one-on-one. This seemed to be really helpful for him academically, but unfortunately, it kept him out of social interactions with his peers where I also noticed that he struggled as a minority.

Social Struggles

I noticed that Marcus exhibited the minority effect on the playground as well as in the classroom. I often observed him wandering around alone with his shoulders slumped over, and he looked rather sad. Sometimes, he would even come up to me and tell me that he was bored because he did not have anyone to play with. When I asked him why he did not try to initiate interaction with other students, he would say things like, "They don't like me," or "They don't want to play with me." I did not think that this was actually true, because I knew that many of the white students played with minority students on a regular basis. I had a feeling that he thought about his troubles on the playground in much the same way that he thought about his academic problems and thus attributed them to being racially different than the other students. I wanted to help Marcus see otherwise, so on one occasion, I asked him why he thought the other students did not want to play with him. After some prodding, he admitted that he was often mean to his peers and did not play by the rules of the game they were playing. We discussed why those actions might make his peers less inclined to include him in their games, and I pointed out that the issue was his behavior and really had nothing to do with him as a person. Fortunately, I pointed out that his behavior could be easily modified. This seemed to encourage him somehow, and he ran off to play.

Reflections

As I look back on Marcus's situation, it makes me very sad that he had such a discouraged attitude in the classroom and on the playground due to his status as a minority. It appeared as if he had given up on his chances for academic success and friendship simply because he was racially different than the other students. His situation showed me in a very concrete way how race can affect a student's overall experience in school. I am very glad that I had the opportunity to talk with Marcus on several occasions and explain that being different did not mean that he was any less capable than other students or that he could not have friends. I think these discussions, combined with his teacher's special attention, made an impact on him, even though it may have been small.

Unfortunately, I think Marcus's experience is very typical for minority students, and students in my classroom will likely have feelings very similar to his. From my own experience being a minority in the classroom this semester, I can see how being a minority brings on social and psychological issues that easily distract a person from learning experiences in the classroom. Given that as an adult I struggled socially and psychologically with being a minority in the classroom, I imagine that my middle school students will have even greater difficulty. It is easy to sit in the classroom thinking about how out of place you feel or worrying about what other people might be thinking, and before long, you have no idea what the teacher has been discussing.

Despite my ability to sympathize with minority students after my experience this semester, there is one big difference in my experience with anxiety over being a minority in the classroom and what my students will likely experience: I am a member of the majority race in society, and I am unaware of any stereotypes that suggest that I would perform poorly in comparison to minority students. Thus, even though I am a minority in my class this semester, I still have the overall mind-set of being a member of the majority because I am white. There are no stereotypes about poor performance that I am likely to fall into. On the contrary, the stereotypes that most likely weigh on my subconscious mind are those that tell me that I will perform better than my minority classmates. Thus, while I have felt social anxiety in my class, I have still been able to perform well academically.

FINAL REFLECTIONS AND SUGGESTIONS FOR TEACHING

Knowing that my minority students will be facing social anxiety and issues like stereotype threat, I realize that it is very important for me to work hard to make them feel comfortable. Although I am not currently teaching, I have a few ideas that I will implement once I am in the classroom. One idea that I have from my own experience is to be careful not to focus my attention too much on any one student. Just as I began to feel that my professor was staring at me this semester, I am sure my minority students may feel that I am constantly watching them if I am not careful to continually move my gaze from one student to the next.

I will also utilize activities that cause my students to get to know one another. If students get to know one another, they will probably find common interests and realize that they are not so different. I think I would have felt less out of place this semester if I had been able to really get to know some of my peers. Students often group themselves by ethnicity if left to themselves. Therefore, teachers can facilitate interaction between students of different ethnicities and create situations that will specifically help them to learn about one another. Having relationships with the people around you can create a sense of comfort and familiarity rather than the feeling of loneliness and misunderstanding by others.

Overall, my experience as a minority in the classroom this semester has been a very valuable one. Though I am white and cannot fully understand what it feels like to be a true minority in this country, I have been able to experience the feeling of being self-conscious about my race. I hope to use my experience and strategies I am learning in this course to make my classroom a place where minority students can feel comfortable and be successful.

IV

SHORT NARRATIVES OF DIVERSE MINORITY EXPERIENCES

20

It's Eleven Thirty at Night, and Da Club Is Jumpin'

MATTHEW REID

As I ate a late after-church lunch with my friend Collette, many ideas were spinning around in my head. I had a wonderful experience in her church and congregation, but this experience wasn't eye-opening, unique, or particularly insightful for me. I wasn't sure if it was the fact that I had worshiped with several African American congregations in the past or that I felt so comfortable in my surroundings. Nevertheless, I truly felt that the church experience was not a significant enough cultural plunge; I had not truly felt what it meant to be the "other" that day.

I was thinking that the most significant minority in my classes was certainly African American, and I knew that this was the community that I wanted to observe in order to better serve my students, but a church setting just didn't seem quite right. This was when Collette dropped the bomb of inspiration! Her friend often went to an African American club in Winston, and she thought that I should check it out the following weekend. "Why not?" I thought. Perhaps this was a legitimate opportunity for me to take a deeper cultural plunge. After all, isn't a hip-hop club a race-based formal gathering?

I thought that the club is a cultural gathering where I could observe a minority group in a setting where they are the majority. I hoped as well that, with the aid of some cultural music and a bit of cosmopolitan social lubrication, I might witness firsthand an African American cultural perspective in which I could get a true feel as an outsider. After all, the social aspect of being a minority in the classroom is at least as significant as the formal aspect, and hopefully, I could gain an insight into how the minority student feels in my classroom and, as a final goal, learn how to change my classroom environment to be more accommodating to my minority students.

At the Club

I decided to go alone to the club—something that I rarely ever do—since, on the few occasions that I go out, it is usually with a group of friends. As I pulled up in the parking lot, I saw a group of guys standing outside waiting to get in. They went silent as I approached and then carried on with their conversation, not caring too much that their sideways glances might be making me uncomfortable. I went inside, bombarded with the thumping beat of hip-hop music and the cloying stench of cigarettes.

Wandering through the dimly lit bar, I felt that I was beginning to experience being a minority. There were looks, sniggers, and the feeling that they all thought I was some rich white boy looking for a bit of "thug" for the night. It was at this point that I began to consider how I often viewed the minorities in my natural social settings. Do I make them feel uncomfortable? Do they feel that I judge them by my glances? Do I flash looks that clearly communicate to them that they are onto some hidden agenda that is apparent solely by their presence in a place where they clearly are the minority? I had to admit that, very likely, this was true. The advantage of choosing this venue instead of a church for my experiment was that I, at least, was able to imbibe some cold beer from a slightly cold barman. At this point, I decided to wander through, in order to take in more experiences.

The air was thick with the heart-pounding thud of the bass and the piercing vocals of a rhythm and blues (R&B) goddess I had never heard of. I was taken by the fact that nobody was talking, but simply dancing or watching others dance. It was at this point that I understood what it meant to be a part of a demonstrative and high-context culture, where nonverbal communication reigned supreme. Although improbable, the people here appeared to know each other and didn't have to talk to communicate. Even those who were certainly strangers to each other seemed to speak the same language: the language of subtle expressions and often provocative dancing.

After acclimating myself to my surroundings, creating a connection with one of the lone dancers became my highest priority. Here again, I noticed the high-context elements of the evening. Nobody really wanted to talk. I exchanged pleasantries with a few people, though it became apparent that the language of dance would be the best communicator. Though I would certainly fulfill the "white boy who can't dance" stereotype, I was determined to try. As I edged toward the dance floor, I became quickly aware that my dancing ability wasn't going to be important: a tall, lanky guy wearing a doo-rag and a gold grill (tooth jewelry) stopped me in my tracks with a "'Sup, boy!" This was the extent of our introductory conversation as he led me to the dance floor, and we began moving rhythmically with the music, all conversation suspended.

I discovered later, over a cup of coffee at the Waffle House, that this young man, Stephen, was an interesting study. This classifiably "thug-looking" guy in doo-rag and grill turned out to be a law student at Wake Forest University. He explained, in more grammatically correct English than I can muster, that although his family is wealthy and he went to a private school with mostly white students, he still felt a cultural need that was satisfied by "hanging" with the folks "at da club." The doo-rag and grill were recent purchases, and the ethnic slang was discarded as quickly as it was picked up, in a true bicultural fashion. He had immersed himself in white culture but was able to function and ease his way between both black and white cultures.

REFLECTIONS

From the dancing styles to the music and drink choices, the club experience really provided me with a slice of the minority experience. What it did was give me some level of understanding of the social experiences that minorities undergo when attending a school where their cultures are not represented. From the bus to the cafeteria to the school dance, these students are put through a wide range of social settings where they are the minority. I feel that my foray to the club adequately re-created some of these feelings for me.

At the club, I felt strange, foolish, and a bit frightened at first, I must admit. Being the only white person was tough, but I wasn't alienated for long. When I did make a connection, it was as genuine as those that they were making with each other, which was somewhat surprising. However, there was some code switching of languages noted among several of the clubgoers when they spoke to me—from colloquial Black English to Standard English. Certainly, my law student friend was an expert at code switching. In fact, he was the surprise of the night, for it wasn't that he was an expert code switcher and could move in and out of a number of cultural groups, but that, honestly, he seemed more comfortable with me, the white guy, than he did with his African American friends. He was raised, after all in my world, not theirs. Why, then, did he feel this draw to come back and dip into their world? This draw is extremely fascinating to me and perhaps something that I will need to learn more about. Something else that I realized was that I needed to learn more about the minority experience in my own classroom. I got a slight sense of it, but just how tough it is for minority students, I will never know. However, what I know I can do is to make my classroom safe and free from discrimination. I can, through the occasional "high fives" and references to popular musical stars, hopefully let them know that, though I don't understand everything they are going though, I care enough to equip myself with some knowledge of where they come from.

I understand one thing now better than I did before, and that is the power of high- versus low-context; more involved, less formal versus less involved, more formal cultures. I realize that all of my jargon-filled ranting really may not connect with my minority students: they simply are not listening. Therefore, my immediate change will certainly be to integrate more demonstrative, visual and auditory media into my lessons. I was already a disciple of differentiated instruction, but now I know that my work involves not only aiding the diverse learners to learn but also helping them to feel safe and comfortable. This shouldn't be simply a teacher's goal but a requirement.

21

I Fit in Perfectly with the Corporate Environment . . . Except for My Accent

Joseph Edmonds

I grew up in Huntington, West Virginia. Shortly after graduating from college, I moved to Los Angeles, California, to begin work as an actuarial trainee. I went to work for large life insurance company in south Los Angeles. Coming from a white middle-class family, I fit in perfectly with the corporate environment in terms of appearance. However, the problem that quickly became evident was my accent. This was a complete surprise to me. Coming from Appalachia, the way I talked was more southern than midwestern. Actually, the Appalachian accent is very distinguishable from even a southern accent, It certainly was different from the Midwest-influenced accent found in California.

When meeting a new coworker for the first time, the reaction was always the same: The substance of what I had to say was perfect. However, as soon as I opened my mouth, the accent became the dominant factor. The next question became "Where are you from?" which created the second problem: being from West Virginia, which had its own stigma. As a result, I was quickly put into a group based on how I talked and the place of my birth. This was ridiculous to me. However, I did not make the rules in this situation.

The Consequences of My Minority Effect

Although my minority situation was small compared to that experienced by racial minorities, some of the feelings and reactions were similar. Being in the excluded group, I sometimes would create my own customs and reactions to situations. In some cases, my accent worked to my advantage since I had a unique feature. Nevertheless, it became my primary identity at my job. In all cases, I was the member of a minority group.

As a result of my identification as a minority group, my work became affected. In a corporate environment, career advancement is everything. If I were excluded from the main group of actuarial students, how would I advance to the higher job levels? I felt that I always had to exceed at every job in order to get the same measure or perception of attainment that others received with ordinary effort. I realized that my future prospects were not bright. Would the company promote someone who sounded like he was from the Appalachia? I often wondered.

As a result of these questions, I decided to leave Los Angeles and return to a job in Jacksonville, Florida. The southeastern United States was more in tune with my personality and lifestyle. Suddenly, the midwestern accent was now in the minority at my new job! My career was back on track.

"Acting the Minority" Phenomenon

Several years ago I taught in a middle school in a lower-middle-class neighborhood. African American students made up approximately 20 percent of the student population. This was before the infusion of gangs in present-day American schools. I was teaching a general mathematics class that emphasized basic computation skills. In this class, there were four black students in the class who exhibited the "acting the minority" phenomenon. They took their seats in the back corner of the classroom. While I went over the examples for the class discussion, these students would talk among themselves. Although the talking was not tremendously disruptive, their participation in the class was nonexistent. The classroom appeared to be divided into two groups, with the white students in the participating group, and the black students in the nonparticipating group. The academic performance of the four black students was very poor.

Because the nonparticipation of the minority group let to a poor academic performance, I decided to take action. I separated each of the four students to different areas of the room. Also, I made it a point to involve them and call on at least one of the four each class period. The results were notable. All the grades of the minority students improved immediately. By engaging the students in the classroom discussion, their interest improved. It was important for them to participate in the class as students—not just as minority students.

Reflections on Culture and Comfort

Minority students in my classroom would experience the separation that I felt when I visited a black church congregation. All members of the church congregation were friendly and welcomed me into their service. However, even with the warm welcome, I felt a sense of separation from the majority group. Minority students in my classroom would likely not experience the actively extended warm welcome that I experienced. The friendliness and closeness among the white students would likely not be extended to the minority students. For this reason, their feeling of separation from the majority members of the classroom would be even more pronounced.

The white students are members of a *low-context culture* (Gudykunst & Ting-Toomey, 1988). This means that their communication would be more direct and sometimes appear harsh to the black students who are more likely to come from a *high-context* culture. Also, when called on by the teacher, black students will often avoid eye contact. This compares to the direct eye-to-eye approach for the white students. The lack of eye contact may appear to the untrained teacher as a sign of disinterest or disrespect. Another problem may occur with the verbal communication for some black subcultures in America. Their verbal communication—Ebonics or colloquial black English—may sound like "street talk" to white students or teachers. Because of these cultural differences, minority students in the classroom are likely to feel the separation that I felt at the black church and my California workplace. Even in the friendliest of classrooms, there would be this group separation because of cultural differences.

CONCLUDING THOUGHTS

The primary way to combat the minority experience in the classroom is to engage the minority students in classroom activities. I would also find ways to let my minority students know that they are important to the class. In addition, I would learn information that will make me more proficient in culturally relevant instructional practices.

If I could change things right now, I would insist that students and teachers accept diversity as a wonderful feature of American society. I believe that we should live together as one people and celebrate cultural differences, and never divide society because of our ethnic or racial origins.

22

The Few White Girls in the Dance Hall

TIFFANY ADAMS

There have been many instances where I felt like the minority. One time, I went to a club with two other white girls, and I believe we were the only white people in the whole place. It was my first time there, but the other two girls had gone there before. I felt like I wanted to hide. As opposed to feeling like I stuck out like a sore thumb, I rather felt like a little peon, midget, or something of the sort. I tried to always place myself between or behind my two friends. This was very easy to do since they both are pretty tall. Although it was very dark in there, I felt we stood out like a bright light. At first I noticed that people walked right past without even a glance at us while we stood at the bar.

We proceeded to the dance floor. It appeared packed that night. There was some space on the dance floor, but people were shoulder to shoulder, all around it. My friends saw some people they knew, so we walked over to them in the back corner, against the wall. I walked in the back of the line with my head down so I wouldn't make eye contact. If I needed to look up and accidentally made eye contact with someone, I would give a small grin with my lips pressed together as if to say hello, although I never got a hello or a smile in response. I stayed very quiet and only spoke when spoken to. I was very careful with my every move so I wouldn't trip and especially so I wouldn't step on or run into anyone. My friends, however, seemed very relaxed. They often dated black guys and were very comfortable around African Americans. They found it humorous how uncomfortable I was. I wouldn't even order a drink for myself. I had them do it for me so I wouldn't sound like an idiot and fumble with my money when paying for it.

We then decided to dance. I was very nervous. I love to dance, and I would say that I dance like African Americans. Therefore, I was very careful with my movements. I felt like I was dancing in a tight box. I don't think I ever even picked my feet up. Some guys came over to dance with us, and I felt even more uncomfortable. African Americans, I had learned, like to get very close and give compliments. In retrospect, I now realize that their compliments, or what they call "hollering at," are very direct and straightforward. I used to get uncomfortable, but now I realize they are not trying to be rude but are just trying to give a compliment.

While dancing, I made myself be more relaxed so I didn't seem rude and standoffish, but as I relaxed and brought my head up, I noticed all the glares from the black girls. At the end of the song, I thanked the guy for the dance and went back to my wall.

On our way out, we passed a line of about five black girls. I looked the other way, pretending that I was watching the dance floor. My friend turned back to say something to me while still walking and ran into one of the girls, knocking her cell phone to the ground. She picked it up for her and tried to apologize, but the girl was angry and told her to watch what she was doing. I was so nervous that I tripped over my friend's feet and about ran into the girls myself. My friends just laughed it off.

When we left and went outside, I felt a relief as I got my first breath of fresh air. When we got to the car, I felt exhausted and mentally drained even though we only spent a couple of hours in there.

Teaching Implications

Now that I have experienced being the minority a few times, especially teaching in a school that is about 90 percent black, I feel more comfortable being the minority around a group of minorities. Through my personal experiences, I am now able to better identify with and understand when my students feel like the minority. I now realize how insecure my students may feel in the classroom. I'm sure my minority students often feel afraid to be outspoken. I'm sure they are scared to answer questions in class, knowing it would bring them unwanted attention and all eyes would be on them, as if they were in a spotlight. I know that kind of attention can cause embarrassment. They may also be embarrassed to speak because of their accent or lack of English language proficiency. When children are quiet, especially around African Americans who are typically louder, they appear to be weird—especially if they avoid eye contact and don't answer questions when people speak to them.

First and foremost, I can help my minority students become comfortable just by reading and understanding different cultures myself. I can also find ways to tie culturally relevant knowledge into lessons. I can help my students to feel comfortable with who they are and to take pride in themselves by using different role models in my lessons. While pointing out differences for academic purposes, I would be sure to point out as many similarities as possible. I will help children understand other cultures by reading books and giving different scenarios. By providing children with the knowledge about various cultures, they will understand each other better and will know that although we are different, we are also very similar.

23

A Lone White Female in an All-Black Course

LAUREN EMERSON

During my freshman year of college, there were no available English classes left for me to take, so I ended up signing up for an African American studies English class. I was the only nonblack student in it. On the first day of school, the teacher looked around and asked if anyone did not belong in that class as she read a description of what the course entailed and looked directly at me while doing so. I felt like she was pointing me out to the class and questioning my being there, as if to say that I did not belong there.

Throughout the semester, we often had to get into groups, and as I expected, no one wanted me in theirs, and so I had to be assigned to groups that gave me evil looks and wouldn't let me participate. Once we started writing papers, our first topic for a paper was about what it was like to grow up black in America. I felt like they just left me in the dark as to how to go about writing it and what I should do, and when I asked the instructor for help, she flatly stated that I should "try to assume what black students in your high school went through."

I reluctantly wrote the paper, and the next week, she had us read our papers to the whole class! Everyone stared at me flatly as I read my paper, which was nothing in comparison to theirs, and the looks on their faces reflected that. I almost thought they were smiling and laughing at me. I cried in front of the entire class that day reading my paper once I realized the impossibility of the assignment, and my instructor did not intervene: she just had me sit down while the rest of the class presented theirs. I had never cried in a classroom in all of my K–12 school years, and I could not believe that I did during my first semester of college!

Needless to say, I was very embarrassed, and the other students' opinion of me never changed. The consequence of my experience in that class was that I purposely avoided any class that insinuated that I might be the minority. Besides, I was no longer interested in learning about other cultures if that was the way the classes would be like.

Teaching Implications

Being a minority student would be much more difficult and straining, in my opinion, because these students have no choice but to go to schools where their need for self-preservation outweighs the material learned in class. I can relate to them because it was very hard for me to want to do the school work when I knew it would end up with me being possibly embarrassed or called out.

In school, children are learning about who they are and where they fit in, and if they have a difficult time adapting to their environments, they may feel socially awkward and become withdrawn. In many classrooms, the American values instilled in children reflect how they should behave or what is accepted by the majority. This forces minority students to question their own cultural values, if the classroom environment is not conducive to free expression of ideas and beliefs. Consequently, these students will feel unaccepted because they are different in a class where no one, including the teacher, may understand where they are coming from. Just as the instructor I had during my freshman year did not understand my position in her class, so might other minority students feel that they cannot ask for help and therefore give up on their school work—something that can lead to higher dropout rates among minorities.

One thing that can help minority students is the formation of clubs and organizations that are relevant to things of interest to them. It helps them to find others whom they can relate to and talk to about their struggles, as well as forming healthy identities within their culture and the school environment.

If I could change anything right now, it would be the way school districts and borders are organized. Currently, many schools are grouped around socioeconomic levels, which place many minorities in the same school and all of the white students in another. I would organize schools such that all students would interact and learn about each other so they will grow up to be accepting of other people's backgrounds and cultural differences.

24

A White Guy at a Black Student Union Party

JEREMY LALIBERTE

In the second half of the first semester of my freshman year in college, I had a black roommate of about twenty years old. I spent most of my extra time that semester learning to play spades and getting to know the kids in the dorm, and he spent his at the gym trying to "walk" onto the football team. He and I never became very close, though we were friendly with each other and often stayed up talking about random topics at bedtime.

One weekend night, I had been at a party with some other friends and was walking back to the dorm with them. It was already fairly late, but not so late that I felt I would go to sleep right away, so I expected to play cards in the common area for an hour or two before getting to bed. Closer to the dorm, however, I happened to pass my roommate. We all said "Hi," and I asked him where he was going. He said that he was on his way to a party at the student union and invited us to come along. We had never been to a party together, and I still had fun on my mind, so I happily agreed, and my other friends said they would meet us back at the dorm later. I joined him on his walk to the student union.

Surprise!

When we arrived, I saw the banners indicating that it was a black student union (BSU) party, but it did not occur to me until I entered the ballroom that I might be the only white person in the room. Sure enough, I was! I don't remember what the event was. I only knew that it was a formal BSU affair. Not only was I the only white person, but I was far from dressed for the occasion. Although my roommate was not dressed for the occasion, either, he didn't mind. I nearly completely shut down. I saw all eyes on me. I didn't just feel the eyes; I saw them. Everyone I looked at was virtually staring at me because I had no business being there whatsoever. I looked at my roommate to see if he might have noticed, but he was too busy among the crowds, enjoying himself.

Eventually, I got my roommate's attention and told him that I wasn't sure I could stay. I clearly told him that I didn't think I belonged there. He told me not to worry and to hang out and have a good time. I gave myself about three minutes to see if I could talk to anyone or relax at all. I looked at the dance floor to see if I could at least dance on my own for a bit to try to loosen up, but nobody was dancing. I even checked for liquor, but it was a campus event: no liquor was allowed. Once again, I told my roommate that I didn't belong and that I was going back to the dorm. He laughed and said, "OK," and I left the party.

Reflections

I had never before—or after—felt nearly as awkward as I did during the five minutes I was in that ballroom and was trying to get out of that ballroom. I could barely breathe, until I was outside and away from the student union that night. Any time anybody ever mentions being a minority or experiencing discomfort when someone is different, I think about that night. When I think of claustrophobia, I think of that night.

When I saw my roommate again the next day (I assumed that he had a good night), we didn't even talk about it. I believe he understood why I left and was not insulted. If anything, he might have thought that I had a chance to experience being a minority and that I may have been able to gain a new perspective. It's possible also that he didn't give it a second thought. We continued our conversations as usual. We played cards with others at the dorm. He taught us a card game none of us had heard of before.

At the end of the semester, he borrowed a friend's car and drove me and two others to our homes a few hundred miles away. As I said earlier, we never got very close in our half semester, but I have that one night to remember for the rest of my life.

Classroom Applications

Keeping in mind how I felt in similar situations as an adult, I can imagine what an adolescent minority might feel. For example, if a young Mexican boy who knows little English enters a primarily white high school, he might not want to come back the second day. He would likely be disoriented since he would not understand all the chatter and would not know anyone at the school. Most children would not notice him, but he might think everyone is looking at him. Emotionally, he might become nervous to the point where it shows physically through sweat or shudders. He might try to read minds through interpretation of body language, facial expressions, and tone of voice. This can be a dangerous territory, since misinterpretation is highly likely, having come from a different culture. Laughing might be perceived as insulting, for example, even if it was completely unrelated to him. He would probably be fearful of approaching the other students, as I was in the BSU example. He would likely feel very lonely and would not know how to handle the situation.

One way to help the same boy might be to find a friendly student who can speak at least conversational Spanish to introduce him to the school. If I find this boy in my own class, I wonder if designating a friendly peer mentor on his first day might help him feel invited just as a man who was friendly with me at the black church I visited did.

All students have emotional needs. Minority students have a special set of needs, and we need to know how to help them. I would end by noting that I plan to investigate more ways of helping minority students as I venture into my career as a teacher.

25

Slowly Embracing a Different Taste

Melissa Loftis

During this past year, I had many students from different countries represented in my second grade class. There were students from Mexico, Ecuador, the Philippines, and Asian and Middle Eastern countries. During the third week of school, one new student joined our class from Ethiopia. She was an excellent student who sought after knowledge and worked very hard and tried to make friends. Every time I taught a new lesson, she would do the work, finish the extra work, and ask for more to do at home. She wanted to succeed really badly in school. Each week, she would tell the whole class stories about Ethiopia and about her pets that she missed. She was well liked in the classroom, and all the teachers absolutely loved her spirit and energy.

This description tells only a small part of my observations about Zinga, my motivated Ethiopian student. Occasionally, she felt the weight of the differences between her culture and that of the United States. For example, she was not allowed to attend school dances, performances, skate nights, or pizza nights because her dad would say no or wouldn't drive her. This was very hard for her to understand, but I did talk to her about other games and things she could do at home with her older brother and younger sister so they could have more experiences.

Introducing "Injera"

Zinga's minority experience that I found particularly interesting happened on the day we did a report about our favorite foods. She was very excited to present her description of her favorite food. The class had already heard about tacos, chalupas, pizza, and hot dogs. She came to the front with her picture and report to read to the class. As she started to read, I saw the puzzled looks in the audience's faces, wondering what "injera" was and how it was considered "food" because they had never heard of such a thing before.

Well, Zinga finished her report, not noticing the confused looks her classmates were giving her. She proudly showed her picture and pointed to the sauce and bread within the picture to help us understand her story better. At this point, there were many questions from the class—so many that she had a worried look on her face. This is the same look that I saw before when she couldn't go to a dance and didn't feel like she was fitting in. I calmed her down by letting her know that this food seemed very interesting and new for many of us, and that I (and the class) couldn't believe that she ate this meal four to five times a week and that we have never even heard of it, let alone tried it. I praised her for teaching us something new and asked her to show us the picture she had made along with telling us who ate this and how they ate it. She proceeded to tell us that she and her family all eat out of one bowl, using their hands to dip pieces of bread into the injera, and that the injera was very spicy.

Embracing Injera

Now that Zinga was on the way back up the self-esteem ladder, I asked her if she would ask her parents if they would make a little extra injera for us so that we could all try it at lunch during the next couple of days. She agreed, and three days later we had our first taste of injera as a class. I tried it first, and yes, it was very spicy. Then one brave second grader who decided it wasn't too weird tried it, and surprisingly enough, many of my students found the pita-type bread and the spicy sauce to be tasty and delicious! We as a group made Zinga feel valued and unique by making this experience a happy and accepting one when it could have turned out differently if she had been in a class where the teacher was less sensitive to her.

26

Surviving in a New School through the School Band, but No Drums, Please!

LORETTA SULLIVAN

There have been a few times that I can recall being the situational minority. One time that comes to mind is when I entered a new school in sixth grade. School had already been in session for a couple of weeks, and my family had just moved from Columbia, South Carolina, to a tiny, rural town in South Carolina. I went from a large city school to a small rural school. I didn't know anyone, felt very lost, and was also way ahead, academically, of almost everyone in my grade. The school was less prosperous than my city school and also had a roughly 40 to 50 percent minority population, compared with the lower percentage I recall from my previous school. There were also a much higher percentage of low-income white children in my new rural school.

In my new school, I realized that I had the command of a large vocabulary, including many words that most of my classmates would never have thought of using, and I wasn't afraid to use that vocabulary—a factor that made me feel a little bit superior. I felt that the students made fun of me behind my back because I had a funny accent (I never quite ditched my Ohio accent), and I responded by being weird and silly, in a vain attempt to make them laugh and maybe like me. That didn't work too well, so I retreated to my world of books, which I would read between and during almost every class, except for math. Most of the classes were just repeating the content matter I already knew, and when called on (the teachers could obviously see I wasn't tuned into their lesson), I would ask them to repeat the question, give them the correct answer, and then return to my reading. Math was harder, so I couldn't really afford to tune out the lessons.

On the playground, I was essentially a loner, and the same was true at lunchtime. I felt out of place, awkward, and tried to *appear* totally uninterested in the other students or in making friends. All I wanted was the close of the school day, to hurry up and get on the bus, and go home, because my parents had bought a farm and my lifelong dream: my own horse.

Connecting through the School Band, but No Drums, Please!

After the first couple of weeks at this new school, I found out there was a middle school band and was asked if I'd like to learn to play an instrument. Since I already knew how to play the piano and read music—and my mom was a drummer at school (cultural reproduction at work!)—I thought I would try the drums.

The first day I went to band, though, I saw about eight boys lined up along the back of the band, all with drums and decided that I did *not* want to be back there with all those boys. So I took up the clarinet instead, which is the other instrument my mother played. My ability to read music led to my helping and befriending another girl in the clarinet section, and she introduced me to her friends. After that, I joined a little collection of about five female friends and at last began to fit in. I stayed in the band, with my first friend, all the way through high school. My first friend, Magdalene, dropped out of school when she turned sixteen, to get married. We never found out why she would do such a thing, but I suspect that it had to do with her trying to get out of her home situation, and she used marriage as an escape to do so.

General Reflections

I suppose the consequences or benefits of my "minority" situation included the fact that I at first gained a reputation for being very brainy and smart, since I was academically ahead of the other students. This reputation followed me throughout my academic career and created the expectation that I would always have good grades. (I already had my family expecting me to excel as well.) Therefore, I rose to the occasion and eventually graduated fourth in my class of eighty-eight seniors. I also realize now, that joining the middle school band probably saved my social life, because it finally put me on even footing with the other students in that class. Since we were all new to playing band instruments, it leveled the playing field. This allowed Magdalene and me to be able to establish a friendship because we finally had something in common.

After I made friends, it didn't matter that I was the smartest kid of the bunch; they would freely come to me for homework help. Eventually, the curriculum caught up with me, and I was no longer way ahead of the other students.

One significant consequence from my experience followed me: I eventually majored in music at Florida State University because I wanted to become a music educator. It is interesting how being in a minority situation could have such long-term effects.

Teaching Reflections and Implications

A reflection of my minority experiences makes me more empathetic to the feelings of my minority students. I know that there are some things I must *not* do to my minority students, and that includes making the point of singling them out, based on their superior talents or intellect, which is something that can happen to a token student in an honors class. This actually happened to a student in my English V class in high school. She was the only black student in this advanced English class, and the teacher would always call on her for answers, over the rest of us. Then, she would heap lavish praise on her, saying, "That is exactly right, exactly right!" every time, without exception. The rest of the class eventually resented this student, and some called her "Miss Exactly Right" behind her back, because the teacher showed so much favoritism. I felt sorry for her, but never really understood the issues, until now. It must have been an awful experience for her.

I would guess that most minority students have feelings of isolation, apprehension, fear, anger, and a host of other negative emotions, multiplied by raging hormones and fueled by cultural attitudes. Since I'm older, I don't have any more raging hormones, and my cultural attitudes are a lot more developed and informed. Having more knowledge goes a long way toward overcoming all those negative emotions and also gives a person more of an idea of what to expect, as well as what they are entitled to. Minority students are entitled to fair treatment and as good an education as anyone else. They also need to understand that they are not inferior to the other students. Teachers who genuinely believe that all students have strong potential are probably a big key to this: we can work to educate our entire class toward this understanding, that all humans have potential.

I think teachers can keep an eye on student interactions and perhaps "trap" them into ways of getting comfortable with each other in the classroom. When I was new in sixth grade, I got to the point where I felt I had to *act* as if I didn't want to be included in the students' social circles. Fortunately, a teacher encouraged me to join the band, and it suddenly connected me with the other students. I found myself unwittingly interacting without putting on any fronts, because the activity was something I was very interested in. Perhaps, if I can find some ways to remove barriers by making students focus on what they have in common, the students would have more opportunity to establish relationships, thus giving the minority students a chance to feel like they are a part of the whole, rather than sticking out like a sore thumb. Feeling like you belong is a big deal with adolescents, so I think finding ways to help them feel this way would go a long way toward making them more comfortable in the classroom.

If I could change something right now, the change I would most want to see is my accumulation of more knowledge to promote minority confidence and self-esteem. At the same time, I would also want to overwrite (in all of my students) the propaganda of white superiority and replace it with an acceptance of equality for everyone. That is a change that is doable and worth pursuing, even if it is not easy. It's a good thing I like challenges.

V

CONCLUDING NARRATIVES AND ANALYSES

27

Lessons Learned from My Minority Experience

ANN WRIGHT

What a great experience! It would be a farce to imply that I was not uncomfortable at all as a white person attending the worship service of a black congregation, but I consider the experience to have been very positive. Reflecting a bit of cowardice on my part, I asked a black friend, Pat, if I could attend church with her one Sunday and gave her the background of my assignment; she readily agreed. Justifying that action, I decided this small bit of cultural capital (taking advantage of my social connections) is not too different from a minority student who enters a classroom where he has a friend or two of the majority race. It definitely eased some of the nervousness I felt.

EXPERIENCING SALVATION BAPTIST CHURCH

How subdued (I hate to say *dull*) my home church service seems after attending Salvation Baptist Church! The service began with very lively music from the choir, accompanied by an organ, drums, and a tambourine. The choir was much like the stereotypical depictions of black choirs in contemporary movies, with lots of movement, swaying, clapping, and a lead singer with backup from the rest of the choir. The congregation obviously enjoyed the music and participated in various ways—some standing and clapping, some waving hands, and others who remained seated but were clapping or just moving with the beat. I took cues from Pat and her husband, John. At any rate, the opening music was great and proved a reliable indicator of the rest of the morning (and into the afternoon!).

The service reflected the high-context culture attributed to African Americans, incorporating demonstrative body movements, sound levels rising (to a rather loud level), the excitement of leaders, a very animated and loud style of preaching, and much encouragement for the pastor in the form of congregational voicing of "Amen," "That's right," and other responsive phrases that implied agreement with the message. The pastor related stories from his own past, stories of others he knew, and stories from the news. He verified with the church members that they knew exactly what he was talking about with the mistakes people make in their lives and the difference between right and wrong choices. If he wasn't receiving enough affirmation from the congregants, the pastor solicited it with "Can I have a witness?" It was very energizing, and two hours passed without me looking at the clock! Half of the congregants in my little low-context Anglo culture church would have expired from boredom long before the two-hour time frame was up. However, my fellow congregants would have been sorely challenged to do so at Salvation Baptist.

Thinking about Classroom-Church Connections

So how does that preacher's style comment on what African American students may crave as far as an instructional delivery from a classroom teacher? Some reflective questions may be instructive: How *demonstrative* is the average teacher? How engaging or interactive is the typical teacher? Are varying sound levels utilized in delivery of a lecture? Is movement utilized by the teacher as part of delivery? When appropriate, is the relating of a story an integral part of making the point? Is the message delivered on a fairly personal level?

Taking cues from the black minister's delivery, we can assume that African American students are used to, and might prefer, a teacher with a *lively* and *demonstrative* delivery. Initially, I thought, "Well, who wouldn't?" I found the minister's delivery to be engaging and positive. However, I wondered if a very reserved person might find it annoying or undesirable. Coming from a family environment that I consider rather high context, I found it easy to adjust to the black minister's style, but I can imagine that some reserved listeners (regardless of race) might have issues with loud volume and may even find the speaker's movements to be excessive and distracting.

Another significant characteristic that I quickly recognized as an obvious difference between typical black and white worship services is the level of *interaction* between the pastor and congregants. It is OK—in fact, it is preferred—to speak out with a reaction to the message, the idea of call-and-response style of preaching. It would be easy to decide, "Well, that's why black students talk while the teacher's talking; that's what they do in church." Upon examination, though, the responses that the pastor receives are all one- or two-word affirmations agreeing with and encouraging him. Not quite the same as the chatter that often goes on in classrooms during classroom instruction! Depending on a teacher's style and the particular students in the class, it might be productive for her to develop and encourage a similar type of response system where students give either nonverbal or very concise verbal indications of understanding and agreement with the information presented by the teacher. As a preservice teacher, I'm assuming that this kind of interaction happens naturally between a good teacher and her students—reading nonverbal cues and postures, as well as using a variety of techniques to quickly verify that the students are *getting it.* Actually devoting conscious effort and time to develop that kind of system in cooperation with the students could add another dimension to it.

The minister at Salvation Baptist obviously realizes the importance of relating personal experiences and telling stories to make a point stick. That *analogic strategy* also promotes a relationship between the storyteller and his listeners. Teachers understand the challenge of choosing the right stories and experiences to which *all* their students can relate. That requires thought and knowledge of the individuals in the class. Comparing the minister's style and a teacher's instructional delivery to a class of diverse students, it seems appropriate to summarize that it's desirable to have a varied delivery—one that includes changing tones and levels of loudness, movement, and different methods of interacting. The variety should provide something that appeals to all types of listeners—those of both high- and low-context cultures.

Reflecting on how it felt to be the minority in the worship service I attended at Salvation Baptist, I will say that I definitely felt conspicuous—although I also felt welcome (and that helped offset the conspicuousness). Although I am not 100 percent rhythmically impaired, I cannot claim to be the most coordinated girl in town. So, I had to expend some effort just concentrating on my clapping in addition to constantly checking the bulletin, while simultaneously wondering if others were wondering why I was there. I guess that's the theory of allocation of resources in action! (This theory implies that when people are multitasking on serious tasks, they cannot excel in any one of them.) I felt rather clumsy and self-conscious.

At my church, most members dress casually; at Salvation Baptist, the majority of the congregation (both men and women) dress their best. To be honest, I expected that would be the case, and I had taken care not to look like a slouch. There were lots of dressy suits, beautiful hats, and coordinating purses. Attire adds another dimension to the phenomenon of fitting in—or not.

Connection with Members of Congregation

As I mentioned, having a friend—or a guide, so to speak—within the congregation of the church I visited did ease some of my apprehensions of looking foolish because I did not know what to expect or what was required of me at different points in the service. The congregation was warm and friendly; there was absolutely no difficulty engaging anyone because they were already engaging me. From the time I entered the vestibule, ushers greeted and welcomed me. Other members also spoke and smiled. Those whom I greeted quickly responded with a smile and greeting. The overall atmosphere of warmth and kindness eased my discomfort. It was probably my imagination that some folks had this question written on their faces: Why has this white person come to worship with us today? Doesn't she know this is a black church? To relate this feeling to possible school situations, it is easy to imagine that students can feel conspicuous in certain situations—including cases where that feeling may not even be warranted. The feelings can be the result of real or perceived differences from others—related to race or ethnicity, socioeconomic status, ability or comprehension level, and so forth. Creating an environment in which students feel kindness, warmth, and acceptance can do much to alleviate the discomfort that students may feel because of perceived differences or inadequacy.

When Pat had to leave the church service with her grandson, Barbara (whom I had just met) made sure that I knew where in the bulletin to find the responsive reading. Barbara is apparently one of those people who find it natural to look after folks who are guests or who might find themselves in new situations. Initially, I thought of describing Barbara with the term *motherly*, but that implies that her helpful quality is a female characteristic. On the contrary, this helpfulness should be viewed as a unisex quality. Though I am a preservice teacher, I have noticed during classroom observations that there are students who are much younger versions of Barbara and take the initiative to offer assistance to others. Other students—if cultivated—can also develop that gift. In either case, these students (those who have an innate knack for helpfulness and those who can be cultivated to identify need and offer assistance) are hidden assets that the teacher can and should use to the advantage of her classroom. Students should be encouraged to create a cooperative environment that will enhance their learning in the classroom and lead to their development as productive citizens in their communities.

The Salvation Baptist church members were very cordial to one another—the type of intimacy and friendship that I am used to seeing in a small congregation (such as my own) who worships together on a regular basis. I did not expect that exact treatment because they don't know me, but I did feel that I connected with them through our shared faith. Maybe it is because I tend to be a positive person, but I focused on the similarities (rather than the differences) I found between my own worship experience and that of Salvation Baptist. Teachers can contribute to acceptance and tolerance among students by helping them to focus on the commonalities shared within that community of students.

Standing Out as an Interesting Shade of Red

There were a couple of surprises during the service I attended at Salvation. One of the surprises occurred when the pastor recognized several visitors, including representatives of The Gideons International, who had come to speak at the service. After he recognized them, I didn't realize he was looking at me and was expecting me to stand. By the time my friend nudged me to stand, I had become a focus for quite a few people; I was no longer as white as before but rather an interesting shade of red when I finally stood. A second surprise occurred when I found out that this is a congregation that *marches* to give their offering. When my friend whispered to me that we would be marching for the offertory, I wasn't exactly sure what that entailed and was a tiny bit concerned because I don't know any marching steps. She assured me that I only needed to follow Barbara and all would be fine. She was right; the choir sang an incredibly upbeat song and beginning with the back, the occupants of each pew successively followed as the ushers directed us, went through the line, and deposited our offering in a special container. Luckily, I was not required to know any fancy march step but only had to walk along in a line with everyone else—blending in fairly well (with the exception of my white face). A totally new experience for me! I found this method of collecting the offering to be very interesting, adding quite an importance (and spotlight) to the giving. Wonder what would happen to our level of giving at my church if we implemented the marching procedure?

TEACHING REFLECTIONS

Reflecting on the experience of attending Salvation Baptist, I realized that there are several things teachers can do to facilitate the schooling of minority students.

- *The importance of the familiar.* I realize that I actually had much more cultural capital than just my friend. Being brought up in the church has given me familiarity with such things as responsive readings and litanies, the collection of offering, and other parts of a worship service. Though Salvation's service was different from any I had attended before, there were enough similarities that I was comfortable with the overall process. As students pass through various gateways in the school system (entering a new school, leaving elementary and going to middle school, leaving middle school to enter high school), they may find themselves unfamiliar and uncomfortable with many aspects of their new environment. It is an important part of a teacher's responsibilities to ensure a classroom environment in which all students feel comfortable, improving their chances of higher achievement levels.

  I believe that when a student first walks into a classroom, she makes some spontaneous mental notes about the makeup of the class and the overall environment. She then makes an assessment of where she personally fits into that setting. It's a very early estimate of *How's this going to go for me? What do my chances for success look like with this group?* The higher the maturity level of a student, the more likely she is to realize that she has to give the environment a chance and that this very early estimate of success can be changed by many factors—including the amount of effort she is willing to expend to fit in. The immature student may make judgments and adopt a permanent attitude about the environment before giving it a chance and may also tend to separate herself as a protection mechanism to keep from experiencing rejection. Therefore, it's very important for the teacher to create an environment, from the student's very first footstep into the room; that will swing the pendulum in a favorable direction for each student's first impression.

A minority student could easily feel disadvantaged on the realization that he appears to be different (at least superficially) from the majority of the group. As I did when I walked into the black church I visited, students probably wonder if they have what it takes to accomplish what is required in a situation where they may be different from almost everyone else in the group. I can imagine a Latino student sizing up his newly introduced, white female teacher. *What does she know about me and my people? Is she going to expect me to know the same things that those white guys over there know? I'm doomed.* Or, perhaps the economically disadvantaged student who has only one or two outfits decent enough to wear to school is almost totally consumed by her imaginings of the condescending thoughts of the students and faculty who dress much more prosperously than her. She never contributes in class and keeps to herself so as not to attract any undue attention to her socioeconomic status.

- *Stress the similarities and celebrate the differences.* As early as possible, the teacher needs to stress the similarities among the students but at the same time celebrate the differences that make each one unique. She needs to prove herself an advocate and communicate her high expectations of all students in the class. Showing an interest in each student on the first day should help ease some of the discomfort and apprehension students feel (just as the welcoming attitude at the church put me more at ease). An additional and necessary ingredient for creating this comfortable and respectful atmosphere in the classroom involves behavior management—specifically how students treat their fellow students. Derogatory comments and actions related to other students (or their culture) are detrimental to the classroom environment and should not be allowed. The classroom is often the first place in which many students are given the opportunity to exercise respectful practices toward cultures unlike their own. Open and honest dialogue should be encouraged. Students should also be trained to examine the intent behind comments; teachers should demonstrate that it is more beneficial to engage in dialogue and educate one another than to become offended and shut down by a situation where no offense was intended.

- *Show interest in and know your students.* Depending on the grade level and whether it is a student's first year in the school, the teacher may be able to gather some helpful background information from student files through a "Who I Am" paper, or other teachers who know a student (or one of his siblings). Such practices can assist in making the personal connection between teacher and students faster but should be exercised judiciously. When requesting information from colleagues, a teacher should make it clear that she wants helpful information to aid in getting to know a student to start things on a positive note. The individual interest accompanied by efforts to involve their families should help give minority students more ownership in their schools and make them more comfortable on campus and in the classroom.
- *Extend yourself with professional development.* In contrasting the worship services of my white church and the Salvation Baptist Church, it could be said that different languages were spoken, figuratively—not a language barrier in the traditional sense of the term, but I did not understand everything, since I do not speak black colloquial English (ebonics). In today's classrooms, the limited English proficient student is a much-discussed topic and continues to present one of the more significantly challenging aspects of education. Bilingual teachers (of English and Spanish) are in hot demand. When a student has limited English proficiency, the inability to communicate with his teacher and peers puts him at a great disadvantage. The bilingual capability of the teacher can somewhat mitigate the difficulties faced by the student. In general, teachers who are willing to professionally develop themselves to meet the needs of their students are better situated to foster student achievement.

CONCLUSION

The Experiencing the Minority exercise was a worthwhile investment of time and energy, pulling together many issues. Though it represents only a very brief time spent in a situation where I was the minority, it is an experience that has provided insight and provoked reflection concerning my minority students. Additionally, it has caused much introspection (and growth, hopefully) surrounding my stance on race, ethnicity, and cultural issues. It was interesting to me to recognize that I feel an embarrassment (or maybe *hesitation* is a better word) when admitting that I am fully aware of the stereotypes related to the black culture—the black choir, the preaching style, the dress. Why is that? Perhaps it is because I am wary that others will consider me prejudiced and think that I accept stereotypes without question and apply them without thought to all people of a particular culture. Or, perhaps it involves a concern that others may think I am incapable of making accurate observations that are separate and distinct from the stereotypes. The reflection and introspection involved with the activities of the "Teaching Diverse Learners" course have helped to solidify many of my thoughts on race and other cultural issues that will positively impact my perspective as a teacher. Ignorance of others exists everywhere. One of the best ways we can combat it is to educate ourselves and engage in open and honest dialogue with our colleagues and our students.

28

Experiencing the Minority at the Local Restaurant

TRACIE S. CLARK

I had a difficult time deciding how to mimic the minority effect because I experience it almost every day of my life. When I go to work, I am the only African American in my department. When I go to exercise at my gym, I am one of very few females in the weight room. When I volunteer at the local elementary school, I am a middle-class person in a classroom full of students who have been labeled as "low income" because of their free or reduced lunch status. Nevertheless, I enjoyed participating in this activity because it offered me the opportunity to operate more consciously as a member of a minority group.

DRAWN BY FRIED PICKLES

I am a fan of fried pickles. While at a meeting one afternoon, a colleague mentioned a small local restaurant that has received attention over several decades for its delicious fried pickles. I told her that I would visit the restaurant that week. She and I discuss cultural issues often, and she mentioned to me that the place is very diverse, so I was excited about visiting the restaurant.

When I first walked into the restaurant, I was shocked. I felt as though everyone stopped talking to stare at me. I was the only African American, and I felt as though a spotlight instantly shone in my face. As I was thinking of the millions of ways that I would seek revenge on my colleague, a hostess approached me. She offered me two seat options: one by itself in the corner and one at a table in the center of the restaurant. I would have been more comfortable sitting in the corner, but I thought about the minority effect activity and sat in the center of the restaurant. My rationale was that I already felt as though I were the center of attention, so I might as well sit in the middle of the restaurant.

After easing up a bit, I realized what my colleague meant when she said that the restaurant was diverse. Though I was the only nonwhite person in the restaurant, I began to see the diversity among what I had initially perceived as a homogeneous group. The wait staff had tattoos and piercings all over their bodies; the table in front of me was full of middle-aged men in starched shirts and khaki pants who appeared to be on their lunch break. At the table beside me were four senior citizens; across the room was a woman with her two children; at another table, four young ladies were seated who appeared to be in their late teens. I began to see that I was surrounded by more than white people: I was surrounded by workers, artists, parents, and grandparents. The same people who initially seemed very different from me now seemed less daunting.

Minding Their Own Business—Or Not

Interestingly, there was not much interaction among groups at different tables. People seemed to have brought their own dining companions and did not seek to engage diners at other tables. In their own clusters, people were laughing, talking loudly, and sampling each other's food. Against the wall was a long, high table with seven barstools where people could sit to eat. The people at the single high table seemed to all talk to each other. Initially, I thought that they were together because of their constant conversations with each other. However, when they began to pay their bills and leave the restaurant, I noticed that they were not leaving together or saying good-bye to each other. The closeness of the bar seating arrangement may have "forced" strangers to interact.

When I established eye contact with someone at another table, I would smile and say, "Hello," but most of the people to whom I spoke greeted me and quickly looked away. The senior citizens at the table beside mine were the only ones that I connected with. I overheard one of the females at the table asking the waiter how to fry the pickles. Her companions occasionally chimed in, in an effort to encourage the waiter to share the mystery recipe. I nosily eavesdropped, hoping to learn the restaurant's secret ingredients. The waiter had no answer, so we were all rather disappointed. Once the waiter left, I leaned over and told the elderly couples that I was hoping that they would learn the recipe and tell me, so I could try it myself. They laughed, we exchanged the names of a couple of other places that had delicious fried pickles, and we joked about attempting to fry pickles at home. Shortly thereafter, the conversation ended. I enjoyed the interaction with them, but if I had not initiated it, there may not have been any interaction between anyone else and me, excluding my waiter. For a brief moment, I felt involved—included.

Surprised

I know that this will sound stereotypical, but I was truly surprised by how loud the restaurant was. A hush seemed to cover the restaurant as I entered, but once my fellow diners realized that I was staying to eat, they resumed their conversations. The high volume caught my attention because my past similar experiences are in harmony with Boykin's (1994) observations. In his research, he noted that the African American homes he observed had plenty of animation: lots of movement and loud talking. On the other hand, middle-class white homes tended to be more quiet and demure. From my experiences, the white people I have encountered have been more restrained and less dynamic or animated. At some of the tables, the diners seemed to be competing to see who could either talk the loudest or be the most nonverbally expressive. Initially, the loudness annoyed me because there just seemed to be too many conversations occurring at once. However, I was later comforted by the idea that I could hear most of the conversations; at least, I knew that they were not talking about me! In general, my experiences with white people are usually in professional settings where spirited verbal and nonverbal displays may be frowned upon, so in retrospect, this experience shattered a stereotype for me.

THINKING ABOUT THE CLASSROOM

I believe that my racial minority students feel a small sense of relief when they walk into my classroom and see that they have a minority teacher. Though I may not meet all of their expectations, we share that initial sigh of relief of knowing that we are not the only ones. My minority students know that they are not going to be asked to represent or speak for their entire race or to reinforce inaccurate stereotypes about their racial counterparts. My presence as a minority may initially invoke relief, but my minority students may also realize that our experiences within the classroom are not the same because of power differences within the classroom. My title as a faculty member allows me opportunities, at least initially, to establish the tone of the class, to enforce class policies and procedures, and to ultimately assign grades. My minority students share my status as a member of a minority racial or ethnic group, but they do not have the same initial power or influence over their classmates or within the college that I do as an instructor. Due to the imbalance in power, my students may still feel alone, alienated, and powerless within my class.

Understanding the minority student's experience and culture are important in developing strategies that effectively meet the learning needs of diverse student populations. DeVito (2004) defined *culture* as the specialized lifestyle of a group of people—including their values, beliefs, artifacts, ways of behaving, and methods of communicating. Banks (1988) stated that minority students "achieve less well in school because the school culture favors the culture of White mainstream students and places students from other backgrounds and cultures at a serious disadvantage" (p. 278). Guy (1999) noted that "people who are socially, politically, and economically marginalized are most affected by the cultural mismatch between the learning environment and their cultural history" (p. 5). The cultures of minority students are often misunderstood, ignored, or discounted in American schools, so minority students are likely to experience *cultural discontinuity* (Irvine, 1990). Irvine explained this concept as a lack of cultural synchronization or connectedness. When teachers and students bring different, and perhaps conflicting, cultural experiences into the classroom, cultural discontinuity may occur. These differences often lead to cultural misunderstandings, conflicts, and institutionalized discrimination (Banks, 2005, p. 7). Ultimately, therefore, cultural discontinuity may lead to student hostility, alienation, diminished self-esteem, and academic failure (Irvine, 1990).

Students who are not part of the established norm may be expected to resist education in mismatched settings. Erickson (2005, p. 49) asserts that in such hostile environments, they "often resist, consciously or unconsciously, covertly as well as overtly." Even as an adult, my initial reaction to this new culture at the restaurant was to be defensive: "You do not care about who I am, so I do not care about who you are. Give me my pickles, and leave me alone!" I can only imagine the number of minority students who walk into classrooms across the country and think, "You do not care about who I am, so I do not care about who you are. Give me my assignment, and leave me alone!" Fortunately, I am a rational adult, so I noticed my reaction and worked through it. I reached out to those around me in order to establish commonalities with others so as to ease my discomforts.

Younger students may not have developed the skills necessary to work through their minority experience or alienation. Educators often give up on them: they suspend or expel them from school before they have an opportunity to mature cognitively and acculturate themselves to both their classroom culture and their minority status. Ferguson (2001) chronicled the experiences of Schoolboys and Troublemakers in an urban, predominantly African American elementary school. Schoolboys were males who assimilated (blended) into their school culture. The Troublemakers were those who defied their teachers and administrators and were continuously reprimanded for doing so. Several of Ferguson's Troublemakers spent more time in in-school suspension programs than they did in their own classrooms. Students like those Troublemakers do not have the same opportunities (time-wise) to learn to establish similarities with their counterparts and contribute to the learning process.

TEACHING IMPLICATIONS

During my experience at the restaurant, I felt a brief instance of what my minority students might feel in my classroom. Unlike my students, I was able to leave that new culture and have the option of never returning. Although I appreciate the option of escaping the minority effect experience, I am thankful to be able to apply what I experienced to my teaching in order to develop strategies that ease the acculturation process for my students. Graves (1967) defined "acculturation" as an individual's process of adapting to a new culture by reconciling his or her experiences in a new culture with those experiences in the individual's native culture or previous experience. My students need to feel both comfortable and competent in my classroom, the new culture, in order to acculturate to my classroom and achieve academic success.

The minority effect experience activity has inspired me to try a few new things with my students:

- *Foster "cooperativity."* First, I will examine the furniture arrangement in my classroom. Whenever possible, I will arrange the seating in a manner that will foster collaboration among the students. I am reminded of the high table with the bar stools where everyone laughed and talked as if they were one large group. When students sit in individual desks that face the front of the room, the focus is on me, the teacher. If the desks are set up as a semicircle or desks are placed together—either in pairs or as islands—students may be more willing to converse with and get to know each other. This offers them the opportunity to look beyond each other's outer differences—which are often influenced by stereotypes. I know that many teachers may argue that the last thing that they want to do is to encourage dialogue among their students, a process that encourages talking and "noise." However, I would challenge them to remember that when implemented effectively, *cooperative learning* environments foster constructive dialogues where students learn from both the teacher and each other. Haberman (1991) noted that good teaching stresses the value of learner input in the educational process. Although I am not sure how I would have reacted if someone had asked to share my table at the restaurant, I do know that I longed for some type of interaction—verbal or nonverbal exchange—with my fellow diners. Perhaps a creative seating arrangement will fill that void for my minority students.
- *Highlight similarities.* Second, I will use more examples and activities in class that highlight the similarities between my students. Instead of polarizing the group, I want to establish a nurturing environment where each student feels valued and comfortable expressing themselves. When I was in the restaurant, I was most uncomfortable when I felt different from everyone else in the room. I do not want any of my students to have that same feeling of isolation and loneliness. I began to feel more comfortable when I saw differences among the white people. Yes, I was the only African American, but I was not the only thirty-something; I was not the only female; I was not the only one with a tattoo. In addition, I felt even more comfortable when I found similarities between myself and the people at the table beside me. I transitioned from feeling like the displaced African American woman to a

fellow fried pickle lover. Once I felt included, I began to warm up to those around me, and I felt more open to the experience. A caring atmosphere and emphasis on similarities will encourage students to see each other as diverse members of one community instead of several distinct individuals operating independently of those around them.

- *Integrate multiculturalism.* Finally, I will actively solicit student help in developing integrative multicultural activities and assignments so that we can openly discuss cultural differences. Establishing similarities is conducive to creating a comfortable class climate, but we cannot overlook cultural differences. We must honor, respect, and celebrate student culture, but we cannot celebrate what we do not know. Instead of relying entirely on my experiences as a minority or becoming overly reliant on multicultural literature, I will solicit student input on how they perceive cultural differences. I teach communication classes that include introduction to communication, public speaking, and interpersonal communication. In each class, we discuss the role of perception and how perception is affected by culture. For example, we may talk about multiple reactions to the loss of a loved one. One person may offer condolences for a loved one who is lost, while another person may offer celebratory remarks for a loved one who has passed on to a better life. Each response may be acceptable to one group of people but taboo to another group. As a result of our ongoing discussions of perceptual and cultural differences, students gain new perspectives and a more complete understanding of societal differences, their roles within society, and their ability to influence or shape the world.

CONCLUSION

Participating in the minority experience allowed me to explore my own varying comfort levels in situations where I operate as a minority. I had to independently adjust to this new, temporary world. As an educator, I learned that my minority students face this situation constantly and need to find ways to adjust to these situations. On reflection, however, I know that I can ease this adjustment process for my students because I can identify with their feelings. Therefore, I am now more determined to design my classroom in ways that encourage student collaboration, foster a sense of community among my students, and implement activities that allow students to explore and discuss cultural differences.

29

The Minority Experience from the Perspective of Students of African Origin

CLIFFORD AFAM

As the number of African students attending universities in the United States continues to grow, there is the need to examine the role of race and cultural background on the educational experiences of these students. This essay is a reflection on some African students' experiences of schooling and the impact of our race, culture, and national origin within the K–16 (kindergarten through higher education) educational environment.

Going abroad, for most students, means leaving their families and breaking away from familiar environments including sociocultural, economic, and other support systems, and this can result in personal and psychological problems (Hayes & Lin, 1994; Pedersen, 1991). Here I will share my minority experience as an immigrant, corroborated by the experiences of two of my immigrant friends.

PARTICIPANTS

Before I immigrated to the United States about sixteen years ago (soon after high school graduation), I lived in a society where everyone looked the same and was treated the same way without categorization or stereotypes based on race, ethnicity, or culture. We were all blacks but had different cultures and customs originating from different places in the region, but none of these cultures or customs was considered inferior to the other. I, like others, enjoyed the richness of our cultures and believed that it was a strength in our society. I do not remember having any thoughts of racism or being a minority in any spheres of life before immigrating to the United States.

Two other people who shared their reflections with me, Grace and Prince, spoke in a similar vein. They immigrated to the United States at a younger age—just before high school—and are presently attending a predominantly white university. As friends, we frequently shared our experiences of schooling in America through telephone conversations, informal interviews, and e-mails. I decided to incorporate their experiences into this essay—with their permission—because their stories were similar to mine. The information provided in this text, like that drawn from other life histories, reflects the interviewees' and my perceptions, recollections, and understandings of our collective experiences. Our stories are borne from high expectations about America that did not materialize.

IN PURSUIT OF GREENER PASTURES

For the most part, the stories I had heard before coming to America typified the greatness of this nation, but we only heard one side of the story. For me, it did not take long for reality to hit home. I had a rude awakening, on my arrival at JFK Airport in New York City, as two white males—supposedly cab operators—asked to transport me to New Jersey airport, which was my next destination. I was charged $120 for the trip, and I provided one $100 bill and one $20 bill to the accomplice sitting on the passenger side of the car who, after a pause, said that I gave him one $10 bill instead of a $100 bill. He told me after I disagreed with his assertion that the American dollar bills are usually confusing to foreigners after their arrival to the United States because they are not familiar with the currency. He gave me back a $10 bill, asking me to replace it with a $100 bill. I obliged after he insisted that it was my mistake. I eventually paid him $220 instead of $120. I knew immediately as I got out of the car and checked my remaining money that I had been duped. It was the beginning of the minority experience.

I believed with all sincerity, based on the stories I had heard while still in Africa, that there were no poor people living in America. Just a few days after my arrival in the United States, I saw people wrapped in thick blankets lying by the curb on the streets of downtown San Diego, California. As I tried to reconcile these two experiences, little did I know that racism and stereotyping exist and that I, too, would be a potential victim in my quest for the American dream.

For African students, people in power are Africans like themselves, and the stratification of society predicated on one's skin color has largely dissipated—even postcolonially—and is virtually nonexistent in many countries. Therefore, coming to America exposed me to a society that is riddled with racism, inequality, and segregation in subtle ways. African immigrants who get situated in urban neighborhoods must deal with racism at its most intransigent and basic types from whites, as well as other people of color. They are often unprepared to encounter the various forms of overt or subtle racism that still exist in America (Traore & Lukens, 2006).

In the next sections, I will use immigrant African students' experiences to explore how these minority students negotiate some of the structural barriers we encounter at both our schools and communities, and the strategies we employ.

CHURCH EXPERIENCES

In my early years in Africa, going to church every Sunday was a norm of the society, and the church was a place to learn right and wrong and the teachings of the Bible. I attended Anglican Church early in my life because my parents were Anglicans, but I later changed to Pentecostal churches in search of salvation despite disapproval from my parents. By then, I was a young adult in my early twenties and old enough to make my own decisions. In America, I visited many black churches, since some of them had similar doctrines with the Pentecostal churches I used to attend in Nigeria. I eventually settled for a Presbyterian mixed-race church.

For the minority experience activity, I attended a predominantly white church with about forty-five congregants. There were no black members in attendance on the day of my visit. On arrival at the church, there were three ushers in front of the church building handing out pamphlets and welcoming church members for the day's service. They portrayed surprise on seeing me. One of the ushers accompanied me to the chapel until I was seated. I noticed that no other white member of the church that came in after me, or at the same time that I did, received this special treatment accorded me. The other church members who were already seated a few feet from me got up from their seats and patiently took turns to personally welcome me to the church before service began. At one time, I thought the greetings were excessive and was becoming a little uncomfortable because I was drawing more attention than I had hoped for.

Some of the church members could not wait until after service to find out more about me. Some said, "I love your accent," and others asked, "Where are you from?" as soon as they heard my accent, which is undoubtedly different. For me, the minority effect emanates not only from my race but also from my accent. It is easy to answer questions about my place of origin, but the questions don't end with "Where are you from?" It is quickly advanced with many other inquiries about my culture and way of life in Africa, including why I decided to immigrate to the United States. After a time, these questions become repetitive, uninteresting, and laborious, especially if I have to do it with almost every person that I come in contact with. For me, it is now a ritual; I have never been angry about it, but I may have answered some of the questions with less enthusiasm. About half of the congregants took turns to talk with me after the service, including the pastor and his wife. The pastor was more measured in his questions and tried not to be overreaching. He appeared to be quiet, soft-spoken, and reserved.

Reflections on the Church Experience

The church service in itself was very short, and I was astonished because I have never been to a church where the whole service lasted under one hour. I was used to services in black churches in America and in Nigeria that last between two and three hours. The singing was scripted, with a live band in session, but did not have the feeling of heavy musical vibration and dancing in black churches. The singing was controlled and conventional. The atmosphere in the church was not in any measure electrifying or moving. The sermon was short, lasting about twenty minutes, and I must profess that it was the shortest sermon that I have heard. The pastor was calm and barely moved, which is unlike most black pastors, who move around the stage, swaying from side to side, and sometimes going down the aisle initiating physical contact with the congregation. It is not uncommon to see black pastors sweating profusely due to the high energy being utilized as a result of their grandiose style of preaching and physical demonstration on stage as they deliver their sermon. Conversely, the sermon as delivered by the white pastor lacked zeal, was nonconfrontational, and was without condemnation based on the teachings of the scripture. Furthermore, although the pastor was not entirely reticent, his preaching style was not forceful but was measured as if his objective was to avoid offending the congregants.

The sermon was largely based on marriage and expectations required of both spouses, but I could have easily categorized it as a short lecture on marriage, based on my spiritual background and experience. I thought that the sermon was elitist, perhaps due to the geographic location of the church and the socioeconomic status of the congregation—which was high-income. The preaching was tailored more toward the rich than the poor—the reverse of most black churches, which model after liberation theology that espouses or interprets the scripture through the plight of the poor and is largely a humanistic doctrine. Black pastors often preach for an egalitarian society and the belief that God always champions the cause of those who are poor and beaten down as they struggle for freedom, dignity, and social and economic justice.

The pastor dressed casually and was wearing long pants and a short-sleeved shirt. He looked like someone dressed for an evening stroll in an elite neighborhood. It surprised me when he introduced himself as the pastor because I was expecting him to be in a suit. It was also surprising to note that none of the church members dressed in a gorgeous way. None of the congregants was formally dressed, including the women. This is unlike the churches in Nigeria and other black churches that I have visited in the United States where congregants put on their best "Sunday" clothes, shoes, and hats, with matching bags.

GRACE'S SCHOOL EXPERIENCES

My perceptions of our time at school as immigrants were similar to my immigrant corroborators, and our narrative sometimes reflected a great deal of frustration. We all talked about curriculum differences but focused more on the differences in interpersonal relationships, the students, and teachers. Grace attended high school in a middle-class neighborhood with predominantly white students and teachers. She noted:

> The school was divided along two streams: the white majority students and the black students, alongside a few Hispanic students. The school was pro-white,

> with a predominantly Eurocentric curriculum. The white students were given passes almost all the time, and the [silly] things they did were seen as "youthful," but the things we did were considered "dangerous" and worrisome. The school never really recognized my cultural background or came to terms with it. My contributions during class discussions were often [either] ignored or elicited negative feedback.

Akbar (1998) said that the American educational system is still structured and built around the identity of whites, and that fosters an increased understanding of their self-knowledge and a simultaneous imposition of an alien identity on people of color. Now, more than ever, American society is very multicultural, and it is long overdue to change the curriculum to include the others. The society has to "embrace the kind of pluralism that offers respect for all cultures and people" because "the educational process can only be effective when it encompasses the cultural uniqueness of the learners" (Akbar, 1998, p.5).

Evans-Winters (2005) noted, "Teachers look for and reinforce achievement-oriented behaviors in white students more often than they do in black students. Teachers are also more likely to give white students praise and attention, and they have higher performance standards for white students than black students" (p.26). It may be argued that Grace was a casualty of a Eurocentric hegemonic structure that had no respect of others' culture—one that mirrored her school's teaching culture. Howard (1999) noted that the responses in our schools have not adequately dealt with the full range of issues presented by the complexities of teaching in a multicultural nation. If Grace's experiences are a tangible barometer of Howard's assertions, then teachers are inadequately prepared to deal effectively with the increasing diversity in our schools.

Grace talked about the constant antagonism between certain groups of students and the minority students. Nevertheless, she felt able to challenge and rebuff such harassment:

> We used to have arguments on sociocultural issues at the cafeteria and during break time. I have been told many times to go back to my country: "If your country is so good, why did you come here?" This was a common theme that I heard from most of the white kids, and it is like they rehearsed it. I usually said that it is a free world and everyone can migrate to wherever they like, including some Americans that live in various parts of Africa. They frequently got angry

> when I told them that the land belongs to the American Indians and that their parents immigrated to America just like my parents.

Stereotyping Minorities

Grace felt that the teachers unfairly stereotyped black students as less intelligent, and did not challenge them enough academically. In their study of black students' disengagement from school, Dei, Mazzuca, McIsaac, and Zine (1997) gave the following account of a student: "It was in the fourth grade. . . . I had a teacher [who] blatantly did not want to teach me anything. And I was the only black kid there in the school" (p. 54). Another student noted, "I don't think the teachers provide enough encouragement towards students, particularly black students" (p. 67). Oftentimes, people of color are left alone in class by teachers to sink or swim by themselves.

Minority students deserve to be engaged in class and incorporated in all class activities like the other kids. The practice of lower expectations conveyed to these students in subtle and perhaps unconscious ways should be discouraged because it does them great harm academically and otherwise. They are subsequently placed in the lower streams and are not encouraged to go into more challenging courses like mathematics or science (Dei et al., 1997). Teachers should encourage students who are passive and marginalized to get involved. Students should not be further alienated because they are black or passive minorities in class.

PRINCE'S SCHOOL EXPERIENCES

Prince experienced problems with some students who found it difficult relating to him. He believes that his accent made the matter worse as it was often used to evaluate his spoken English and the measure of his intelligence. Such stereotyping not only was difficult to overcome but also hindered his working relationship with the predominantly white students.

> I learned that I always had to invest extra efforts in speaking clearly to people because some of the students often tried to avoid me when it was time to do group work. If the lecturer chose the group, I literally had to force for my opinion to be considered. (Prince)

Prince's experience was similar to mine. During my final year in an undergraduate class, I experienced some difficulty finding a group of students to work with in a community health class that required each group to do a poster presentation. The white lecturer sensed what was going on and communicated her disapproval to the students who had turned down my request to join them for the group work. She invited two of the students to her office and had a short discussion with them. Later that day, she told me that she made it known to them that I was capable of contributing intelligently to the group work. I did not consider their behavior toward me as racist, but it was certainly stereotypical, bordering on the belief that I was probably less intelligent due to my race or my accent.

I was confident of my academic ability and satisfied with my grade, but I had no way of telling how intelligent the other students were, since students' grades were private. A mere classroom observation or speculation would have been unscientific. However, I found out during graduation that year from the graduation ceremony pamphlet that none of the students involved graduated with honors. Only two students in my class, including me, out of about nineteen students graduated with honors. Some students socialized with me freely but were constantly asking me rather silly questions about Africa: "Do you have hospitals in Africa?" "How do you live with lions in your backyard?" One of the students asked me if we wore any clothes in Africa. The questions appeared funny at times but in a real sense were absurd. Traore (2006) noted similar stereotypes in an article from her study of African students studying in America. "Familiar images such as Tarzan, savages swinging by vines in the jungle, wild animals, diseases, wars, and starving people were all that the American students at Jackson could talk about when asked about Africa and Africans" (p. 30).

By his first year in college, Prince did not expect a multicultural curriculum within the school. He was not surprised when minorities' experiences were marginalized or ignored. He had resigned himself to learning contexts in which his own experiences and culture were not considered: "Every time I tried to talk about Africa, there was always a feeling of lack of interest. . . . I feel that the interest to learn other people's culture was not there." In their study, Dei and his colleagues (1997) quoted one of their participants as noting that "the curriculum was one-sided, especially when it came down to history. There was never a mention of any black people that have contributed to society" (p. 138). Even when black issues were taught, it was only in the negative. You will never hear Africa mentioned except in a negative light (Woodson, 2000).

CONCLUSION

Immigrant and other minority students of any race can overcome challenges or enhance their benefits from education by inculcating several interventions or changes as follows:

- *The use of social network members comprised of fellow immigrant or minority students as a support system.* Students should have frequent contact with other immigrant or minority students, and this network should be continued throughout the students' enrollment at school. This strategy should include sharing of information on college life, racism as experienced by each other, survival skills, advice for each other, and the provision of encouragement and spiritual support. People feel better when they learn that a certain experience is not unique to them.
- *Forming an organization of (specific) immigrant students with common goals.* Organizing welcome parties for new immigrant students will help alleviate their initial apprehension and fears and enhance their adjustment at school. Immigrant students should utilize these social meetings to speak their native languages and share their culture with one another. These activities will help students overcome the psychologically hostile environment and provide a more conducive schooling environment.
- *The development of equity programs geared toward employing minority teachers, especially, and if possible immigrant teachers and recruiting minority and immigrant students.*
- *The establishment of a group-based mentoring program focused on the development of strategies to deal with minority student issues.* This program should be aimed at dealing with school problems in the context of racism and a Eurocentric curriculum. It should also provide the means by which immigrant and minority students, their peers, and mentors could enter into a dialogue about common points of conflict in school and develop practical strategies to deal with them.
- *Schools and colleges should require every teacher to undergo training on competency in teaching diverse students or culturally responsive teaching.*

30

Experiencing the Minority: Overcoming Double Consciousness in the Classroom

LaTasha Jones

One ever feels his two-ness—an American, a Negro; two souls, two thoughts, two unreconciled strivings; two warring ideals in one dark body, whose dogged strength alone keeps it from being torn asunder. (W. E. B. DuBois, 1903, p. 3)

While growing up, I was in the middle of a school system that sorted people into academic tracks, categorized the worthiness of people, and left me with two warring ideals. This academic system saved and damned me simultaneously as I was both accepted and rejected by my peers. The double consciousness that DuBois wrote about was in my spirit as my one foot was in the higher tracks and the other was in the lower tracks. The higher tracks included my white classmates. The lower tracks consisted of schoolmates who lived in my neighborhood, those I saw when I looked in the mirror. This duality at school caused me to be a mismatch in every school social group. While in class, I was one of the only black students, and my white classmates thought that it was amazing that I could compete with them in challenging class work. On the rare occasions when I visited their homes, their parents said things like, "You're not like those other black people." At the time, I wondered if those remarks were positive or not. For me, they were laden with pain and progress, the same duality that characterized my experiences in my neighborhood, with my people. Even though the black students who lived in my neighborhood viewed me as a *shero* because I had ventured into the unknown—a place that they dreamed to enter but knew did not welcome "their kind"—they did not allow me into their world, either. Even though we shared a neighborhood and a culture, there were so many things that we did not share. In the neighborhood, somehow my race had changed from black to "white." As a result, I formed my own identity that included code switching (speaking both black colloquial English and Standard English) and learning to live in multiple cultures. Sometimes, I lost myself in the process, as I struggled to know exactly who I was in this world of "double life" and consciousness.

AT HOME IN CHURCH

These experiences framed my reference for double consciousness in school, but they contrast with my experiences at my church. I was raised by all of my family—including my black church family. I have fond memories of attending the black church as it was home; it was liberating—it was me. The black church was the place where I found most of my comfort growing up; it was the only place other than my family home where I felt like I could be myself. I was accepted and loved. Role models and mentors pushed me toward success. I was validated and taught black history. The music and preaching styles resonated with what seemed like the yearning within my soul. The environment was always emotional and full of energy, even during portions of the service that were calm and tranquil. The preacher was viewed as the ultimate leader, almost at a level of importance just below God. In essence, he (by the way, our pastor was almost always a male) was a demigod. Even though we were all minorities, in this place, I was a part of the majority and the powerful.

All the churches that I have attended so far reflect my cultural background. There were always elements of call and response or congregant participation—all similar to the communicative patterns used in my home.

Therefore, church was a comforting place for me. As an adult, I have always viewed the church as a solace from a difficult world that continued to impose double-consciousness on me. This caused me to view all churches in a positive light. By extension, therefore, even when I visited churches of different denominations and different demographics, I still felt somewhat at home. I was comfortable not because of the parishioners but more because I knew that the spirit of God was present.

ATTENDING CHURCH AS A MINORITY

The church that I attended was a predominantly white church with about twenty-five members. All the members of the church were white except for the pastor and his family. I thought that it was interesting to have a black pastor and white congregants since I had rarely seen one like this. I reckoned that race was not the factor in determining whether the pastor was competent. It appeared that it did not matter whether he was black or white, but what mattered was that he was placed in a position of power. This intrigued me; I definitely wanted to know more about the race relations within the church and how the pastor's family functioned as minorities in a position of power in a majority context.

Critical race theory (CRT) explains race relations and indicates that because white majority culture is the American convention, whites may therefore view themselves as having no color (Delgado & Stefancic, 1997); they are the "standard" for America's humanity, and racial minorities are subordinate "others." Based on the premise of CRT, therefore, the pastor may be viewed as honorary white because he had been imbued with power and placed into a position of authority—as whiteness is synonymous with power in America. In essence, the congregants "follow" the directives of an African American pastor, contingent on the power they had conferred on him.

Not surprisingly, although the pastor and his family were black, the church experience was not what one would characterize as black church tradition. I was familiar with and had attended black churches that were not representative of traditional black culture. One could clearly characterize this church as white, based on several attributes, from the teaching style of the preacher, to the music played and sung.

Since I have had many experiences where I was the only minority in the room, my experience at this church service was not particularly awkward for me. Besides, I had come here for a specific assignment, and so I chose to view my experience in that context.

Consciousness of Minority Identity

Behavior is dictated by one's consciousness of identity. My behavior while attending the white church was indicative of my consciousness of being black. There are varied ways in which persons deal with identity issues, and William Cross (1991) observed this in his concept of *nigrescence*, which explains black identity development. This concept, which in this essay has been modified to include minorities in general, identifies fives stages of racial identity development, and it can be used as a teaching tool to develop classrooms conducive to minority students' learning:

- *Pre-encounter:* a phase characterized by "color-blindness," whereby individuals may not realize the implications of being a minority
- *Encounter:* a phase whereby some event(s) bring minorities to the realization that they are viewed as the "other" in society and therefore begin a journey to justify their culture to themselves or to others
- *Immersion-emersion:* a phase where minorities mostly socialize with people of their narrow social group
- *Internalization:* a reflective phase where minorities become more inclusive and are open to cross-cultural dialogue
- *Internalization-commitment:* a transcendent phase characterized by minorities' ability to form positive relationships with white people; these relationships are contingent on cross-cultural understanding and insights into the nature of society

Using Cross's model as the basis of reflection, I would place many adolescent students as being in the immersion-emersion phase, and they are therefore uncomfortable when they are the minorities in a given context. This discomfort can negatively impact their academic success (Irvine, 1990). For this reason, it is the task of the teacher to make all students feel comfortable by creating opportunities for student success.

IMPLICATIONS FOR THE CLASSROOM

The experience that I had visiting the predominantly white church is similar to minority students' experiences in the classroom. Even when teachers or students are welcoming in their expressions, their nonverbal cues may be misunderstood. This is not surprising because teachers often do not have the background knowledge to teach in ways that are relevant to students from nondominant cultures (Howard, 2001; Irvine, 1990; Latham, 1999). An area of research that addresses the disharmony between teachers and their students is the concept of *cultural mismatch.* It explains that students and teachers are often mismatched because of inadequate overlaps of related cultures that go along with social constructs such as race, religion, and socioeconomic differences.

Another common area of misunderstanding is the culture of opposition in schools. As a middle school teacher, I observed that there were several types of minorities in my classes, even in a predominantly black school. The "academic minorities" in my classroom were the students who were on the honor roll. These students were very serious about academic achievement but were often ostracized by their peers. One would wonder why minority students may oppose academic achievement. Ogbu (1986, 1991) found that *oppositional culture* is common among minority students who oppose the *ways of knowing* from the dominant culture (compare this with immersion-emersion stages in Cross's nigrescence). This opposition negatively impacts student achievement unless it is countered. Because I knew that my stronger students might be ostracized by their classmates, I made academic achievement a "cool" thing to accomplish in my classroom, for all students. I started out by not only praising the students who excelled but also praising those who took steps toward improvement. This way, all students felt a sense of accomplishment and moved toward embracing the culture of achievement.

Culturally Responsive Pedagogy

Minority students are successful when their teachers implement holistic strategies that encompass curriculum and instruction, classroom environment, and student-teacher performance (Ware, 2006; Howard, 2001) and promote equity and fairness in the classroom (Ware, 2006; Cummins, 1996). *Culturally responsive teaching* (CRT) is a teaching method that can be beneficial for minority students as it includes students' culture and promotes equity in the classroom. Gay (2000) defines culturally responsive pedagogy as "using the cultural knowledge, prior experiences, and performance styles of diverse students to make learning more appropriate and effective for them; it teaches to and through the strengths of these students" (p. 29). According to Gay, CRT has six basic descriptors: validating, comprehensive, multidimensional, empowering, transformative, and emancipatory. Each of these elements will be discussed in further detail in the paragraphs that follow.

- *Validating.* Culturally responsive educators validate their students' cultures. Validation of a student's culture occurs when the student's historical and traditional perspectives are incorporated into teaching and learning. This is very important for students who feel alienated in the classroom. One way that educators can incorporate validation into the classroom is through incorporating cultural role models into everyday lessons. Another idea is by asking the students for appropriate, personalized information. These small acts will help to validate the students and their cultures.
- *Comprehensive.* CRT is comprehensive because it uses "cultural referents to impart knowledge, skills, and attitudes" (Ladson-Billings, 1992, p. 382) while seeking to educate the whole child (Dewey, 1916). Responsive teaching not only teaches academic skills for success but also focuses on other aspects of learning, including social, physical, and heritage aspects of the students. This notion views students as more than academic vessels, but as persons who will contribute to the larger society. One way to foster comprehensive CRT is to incorporate *vision vessels* into the classroom. A vision vessel is a lesson where teachers use goal setting and character education to improve students' current stance. For example, students can be helped to think and research about where they want to be at a certain point in the future, and the steps needed to reach their goals. This type of assignment helps the students to create goals in life, become future oriented, and take concrete steps towards their life goals.
- *Multidimensional.* CRT is multidimensional because it encompasses "curriculum content, learning context, classroom climate, student-teacher relationships, instructional techniques, and performance assessments" (Gay, 2000, p. 31). This gives teachers a variety of ways to impact student learning. The climate of the classroom and the relationship that is formed between teacher and student is included in this element. Teachers can implement strategies to create a warm and caring classroom, including the creation of a *welcome manager.* A welcome manager is a student (of the week or month) who is in charge of hospitality, welcoming and incorporating any new students into the classroom culture. This makes the students responsible for a

classroom culture that is conducive to learning and includes them as coinstructors in the teaching of the "ways of knowing" in the classroom.

- *Empowering.* CRT is empowering and moves students toward personal agency as the teacher becomes the facilitator in coconstructing knowledge with the students. Freire (1993/2000) spoke of the power dynamics inside the classroom. He noted that teachers who intend to share the power with their students do not teach as if students were passive, empty vessels who need to be filled. Rather, such teachers share opportunities to present new knowledge to the classroom *with* their students. Freire and other researchers (Apple, 1996; Giroux, 1997) are of the opinion that teachers are given power and authority by society and must transfer or share their power with students in order to make a significant impact on the academic success of their students.

  One way in which teachers can implement empowerment in their classrooms is by having *weekly reporters*, whereby students give weekly reports of current events in their neighborhoods. The current events can be from various media, including the student media or media club that could be formed in the school or class. The teacher may then incorporate some of their information into various lesson segments. The idea is to empower the students to look for news in their neighborhoods and coconstruct new knowledge with their community of learners.
- *Transformative.* This element asserts that change occurs when methods of CRT are employed. Being transformative involves helping "students to develop the knowledge, skills, and values needed to become social critics who can make reflective decisions and implement their decisions in effective personal, social, political, and economic action" (Gay, 2000, p. 131). When students become social critics, they understand more about society and are able to make positive social change. Assignments whereby students are given the opportunity to use critical thinking skills and assess global effects are especially important when transformation is expected. An investigative action research report is one kind of assignment that would elicit transformation for students. The teacher can require the students to find a research problem and to go through all of the steps of a research method or the scientific process. The culmination of the project can be the sharing of the new knowledge in a community-wide research forum.

- *Emancipatory.* Freedom and liberty are important aspects of CRT. The notion of emancipation expresses the need for students to be responsive to and uplifting of their own communities. Gay (2000) states, "The validation, information, and pride it generates are both psychologically and intellectually liberating" (p. 35). The key in this element is to teach students in such a way that they would be driven to become responsive to and make positive changes outside the classroom. One assignment that integrates this element is making community connections. For example, students may research the health implications of pollution at the local lake or park and involve the community members, including their parents and the local government. Such assignments allow students to find useful ideas or people in their communities who are ready to make positive social changes. The students can connect with community organizers, groups, leaders, and others and form alliances toward self-improvement. This not only helps students become autonomous or agents of positive change, but it also allows the community to enhance civic capacity.

When teachers implement culturally responsive teaching, students coconstruct knowledge and eventually become agents of their own educational experiences (Freire, 1993/2000).

CONCLUSION

The double-consciousness that DuBois (1903) discussed in *The Souls of Black Folk* is a reality for minority students. These students often have "two souls, two thoughts, two unreconciled strivings" that interfere with their abilities to succeed in schools (p. 3). Therefore, it is up to teachers to create a communal, inclusive learning environment where all students can succeed despite their double-consciousness. Culturally responsive teaching is one approach that helps to resolve the challenges involved in minority effect.

31

Comparative Reflections: Lessons Learned about the Minority Experience

CHARLES B. HUTCHISON

The primary purpose of this book is to discuss the natural but rather oppressive human phenomenon that this book refers to as the "minority experience." The minority experience generally leads to a set of mostly negative behaviors hereby called the "minority effect." Anyone who has finished reading this book will probably come away with several lessons or themes about the nature of the human experience, especially when they are in the minority. This concluding essay will make some assertions regarding the minority effect phenomenon, based on the experiences described in the narratives in this book.

1. *The minority experience is a situation-based human phenomenon, and the minority-determining factor may be different for different individuals.* Although physical characteristics such as gender and race cannot be easily hidden, the psychological impact of intangible differences such as religion and class should not be underemphasized. Throughout the book, the authors indicated that as long as there was a means of differentiation

of people in congregations of any kind, they became uncomfortable with their minority status.

2. *The degree to which an individual feels the impact of the minority effect partly depends on that person's (a) previous exposure, (b) interactions, and (c) the subsequent buildup of comfort with, or confidence in, the population in which they are currently operating.* It can be argued that familiarity breeds comfort. For example, in the essay "The Few White Girls in the Dance Hall," the first time Tiffany Adams went to the black club with her friends, she was nearly petrified, while her other white girlfriends were more comfortable because they were familiar with those surroundings. In all the narratives, when the minorities made connections with others, they became more comfortable, and that opened the way for them to connect with others and become integrated. On the other hand, before any such connections were made, people kept themselves apart and wondered about the "other"—the "unknown." This assertion is an important lesson, because it illustrates the fact that when individuals are given the opportunity to learn about and interact with the "other," they are more likely to understand them, allay their "fear of the unknown," and become more comfortable with them. In pluralistic societies, this is a good case for integration at school, work, and residence, but one that is created with intention—*integration by design*; created in such a way that, as much as possible, no one is "left behind" as a minority to suffer its consequences.
3. *The minority effect negatively impacts the social performance of its victims.* Most of the authors behaved in unnatural ways, which made them appear rather awkward, ill behaved, and antisocial. Sadly, these behaviors alienated them from the majority group—the very group whose acceptance and sympathies they needed in order to become included. For example, in the essay "My Dark Curly Thick Hair Was a Nemesis as All I Wanted Was the Blond Straight Hair Parted Down the Middle, *and* Romeo: A Student Misunderstood," Anita McGee became combative; in "A Black Female in a Predominantly White Male Class, *and* Reversing Roles: A White Student Acting the Minority in Class," Lisa McCrimmon may have appeared "nonchalant"; and in "Comparing Experiencing the Minority Exercise to a War Zone Experience: A Soldier's Reflection, *and* Breaking Out in a Cold Sweat in All-Women's Company," Daniel Blankton was obviously antisocial—all in attempts to compensate for their minority experiences. Kalilah Kil-

patrick, in the narrative "Seeing My Student at an All-White Church Saved My Day," made a statement that elegantly conveyed the physicality of her mental state: "I kept my head straight forward in fear that I would not receive a welcoming smile if I established eye contact with anyone. I think my face began to show fear." This statement is powerful because it deftly intersects with Malidoma Somé's question raised in the introduction of this book: What if a newborn cries to be welcomed and there is no response? What happens to its psyche?

The comfort-attraction-success loop. The questions that arise from this discussion include, When people appear awkward or stoic as a compensatory mechanism for being the minority, what is our response? The irony is that such compensatory behaviors are somewhat repulsive of others—leading to the repulsion of potential friends and loneliness. What would happen if the stoic child is helped or eased into the crowds of the comforted humanity? Could her laughter, good countenance, and bright demeanor be contagious and inviting of others? Could she therefore become attractive because she is comfortable? Could it therefore be that the comforted and thus pleasant-looking are more friendly-looking? Are the comforted in a relatively better mental condition to perform better in school and at work? When people perform better in school and at work, are they more contented and therefore look more comforted or comfortable, and are thus more attractive of others? These are interesting questions to ponder.

4. *The minority effect negatively impacts the academic-intellectual performance of its victims.* Most of the authors indicated that when they were occupied with their minority experience activities, they were so self-absorbed that they functionally lost their capacity to think. For example, in "A White Guy at a Black Student Union Party," Jeremy Laliberte mentioned that he "nearly completely shut down" when he realized that he was the only white at the entire function. Another example was in the essay "Experiencing the Minority as the Only White in Church, the Only Woman in Corporate Meetings, and as a Denominational Minority," by Betty Danzi. When in the church, the pastor invited the congregation to open their Bibles and follow along while he read a passage of scripture. She commented, "I had my Bible but found myself fumbling to find the correct scripture reference. I couldn't remember what verse he had just said to find. As we stood up, I was still

turning pages, wondering if everyone around me noticed that I was slow in finding the passage." Whereas the majority of the congregation were operating as a majority does—in their "normal" setting, like fish in water—Betty was functioning like a fish out of water, and was depleting her cognitive resources, gasping for air.

Another archetypal case was Ryan Delehant's essay, "I Already Felt Unwelcome, and . . . This Feeling Was Completely Inside My Head, *and* Stuttering at a Staff Meeting," where the title is self-illustrative. Besides feeling unwelcome and uncomfortable in the church, Ryan noted that he stuttered at a staff meeting, not because he stammered or was inarticulate but because he was too nervous. If his performance was being assessed by his observers as the index of his intelligence and, therefore his academic or human potential, one can only imagine how he would have fared.

The fact that individuals who are experiencing the minority effect underperform academically-intellectually is illustrative of the notion referred to in this book as the *theory of cognitive allocation*. In all of these examples, whereas those in the majority were allocating most, if not all, of their mental (cognitive) resources to the performance of their normal functions without any concerns about who they were—and therefore doing well and *appearing* more intelligent—minorities like Jeremy, Betty, and Ryan were operating like fish out of water that needed to breathe out of water but still function as if there was nothing wrong.

5. *On rare occasions, the minority effect can positively impact minorities' performance, not necessarily because of their increased intellectual output but because of an increased determination to prove one's worth.* For example, in "Black and Female in an All-White and Male Math Class, *and* Mercy's Dilemma," Ora Uhuru "refused" to give her adversaries the "satisfaction" of failure by dropping out of the class; neither did she "want to stereotype [her] race or [her]self by giving up." Ora realized that this determination called for extra efforts on her part: "So I did the next best thing: I asked one of my best friends who was a math major to tutor me. I wanted to shine and stand out among the rest of the students. In order to do this, I had to know everything before class started so I could just follow my teacher's lectures for reinforcement."

Another example of an increased determination to prove one's worth was illustrated by Betty Danzi's "Experiencing the Minority as the Only White in Church, the Only Woman in Corporate Meetings, and as a Denominational Minority." What is remarkable about this narrative is its stark comparison with Ora's. Like Ora, who noted that she "refused to give [her classmates] the satisfaction" of dropping out of the course because she felt that she was representing her race, Betty did not want to fail and "felt that [her] performance had to be outstanding because, in a way, [she] represented all women in the workforce." Ora felt the pressure to succeed in a class where students were ready to mock her if she faltered. She stated explicitly, among several points, that "it took a lot of energy on my part just to walk into this class, not to mention the hostile atmosphere that surrounded me," and also that it "took a lot of courage and willpower" to succeed in that class. Similarly, Betty felt the "pressure to prove" that women are at least as competent as their male peers. For both women, their success came at a cost because, in Betty's words, "I remember spending a lot of energy getting myself mentally ready to meet each new client. It was exhausting."

6. *The effects of the minority experience can be complex and have to be addressed as such.* The very idea of being a minority is rather ironic: It is a complex situation whereby the majority's "silent attention" is drawn to the "other," the minority who oftentimes wants to "hide" within the crowd. The irony is that this person is in a situation whereby the comforting act of another is very much needed, but such an act would explicitly indicate that he or she is a minority and therefore raise the awareness of the person's token status. For example, many caring instructors of lone minorities in classrooms are often confused as to whether or not to recognize and make this person comfortable, or just let that person remain incognito by keeping quiet and "vanishing" in the back corner of the classroom. In Loretta Sullivan's narrative, "Surviving in a New School through the School Band, but No Drums, Please!" "Miss Exactly Right" received negative attention because the teacher made her minority status the obvious reason for the attention given her. However, in Lisa McCrimmon's "A Black Female in a Predominantly White Male Class, *and* Reversing Roles: A White Student Acting the Minority in Class," her instructor was able to balance the provision of needed recognition and attention with sensitivity, leading to her enjoyment of and success in the course.
7. *Conscious, sympathetic individuals can mitigate or even negate the negative effects of the minority experience.* In each case across the narratives, pastors

or members of congregations who were compassionate made the visiting minorities feel welcomed and comfortable. Besides, teachers who were sensitive to the minorities' experiences and took the proper actions to make them comfortable had a positive impact on them. For example, whereas Lauren Emerson felt unsupported by her instructor in her all-black English course and therefore subsequently actively avoided cross-cultural experiences (as described in "A Lone White Female in an All-Black Course"), Lisa McCrimmon felt supported by her instructor in the all-white course (in "A Black Female in a Predominantly White Male Class, *and* Reversing Roles: A White Student Acting the Minority in Class"), and the instructor even went to the extent of using her input as cases for discussion. Having been given a valuable voice, she noted:

> One day after one class, a white female approached me and said that she didn't understand a lot of the cases until she had opportunity to hear my interpretation in class. . . . Consequent to these dynamics, I ended up getting an A in a rather difficult class. I believe, in part, that it was because I was placed in a position to offer a different viewpoint than what was "norm" in classroom discussions, thanks to a good instructor.

She felt valued—and therefore comforted and included—in class. Thus, it is no surprise that she not only did well in this course but also enjoyed it, even as a minority!

COPING STRATEGIES

So far in this book, common behaviors of conscious minorities have been illustrated. This section will focus on common human reactions to their minority experiences.

In school or society, people who find themselves as the conscious, situational minorities use one or more coping strategies to escape or ease their burden. The strategy used is likely to depend on (1) the prevailing conditions and whether they feel "trapped," (2) what options exist under the current circumstances—and whether there are other situational minorities available, and (3) whether there are easier avenues for achieving comfort. These may include the following:

- *Low-profiling (or attempting to "vanish").* As noted in the introduction, one way for conscious minorities to manage their situation is to become *invisi-*

ble in the group context, especially when they feel uncomfortable but "trapped." By sitting in an obscure location (e.g., the back of the classroom in school), they escape the visual field of most observers. To shorten their time span of visibility, whenever possible, they would take the first available seat when entering a room (e.g., people often sit close to the door as if they are ready to escape the discomforts of the group if they could). After having sat, people would often slump (which, in practical terms, involves an attempt to fold over) in their chairs, which means that they are inadvertently trying to physically shrink their bodies in order to become less visible. Such actions give a psychological sense of escape from the present physical and psychological circumstances. Unfortunately, it may also mean that if the conditions in the current environment—be it the classroom or the work environment—are not conducive to optimal performance, the situational minority would be more concerned with vanishing than performance. The likely result is underperformance.

- *Hypervisibility.* As opposed to those who have the opportunity to escape their situations by vanishing, there are situations where the conscious, situational minorities may realize that they are obviously visible anyway. In such circumstances, some may opt to compensate for their situations through some kind of performance. Ironically, since their cognitive machinery is already overtaxed (as illustrated in the narratives), they may make rather rash decisions and end up making a fool of themselves. In the classroom or work context, such individuals may become the clowns. In this context, however, clowning is an unconscious means of redirecting attention away from oneself—or, better put, from one's *self* or personhood.
- *Blending.* There are situations where conscious, situational minorities may have the option of just blending in and therefore achieving invisibility. There are two common types of blending:

  Assimilative grouping. In this situation, conscious, situational minorities eliminate their personal, differentiating characteristics and blend in with the current, dominant environment. For example, individuals may learn to speak the dominant language form, wear the same clothes, and watch the same programs in order to become a part of the in-group, even if temporarily. For example, many African Americans are fluent in both the Standard English and African American Vernacular English (AAVE), but they speak these forms of English in specific social settings. During school

> conversations, students may use the "in" words in order to feel a sense of inclusion, although they are less likely to use such language with their teachers.
>
> *Homogeneous grouping.* When conscious, situational minorities find others like themselves in the environment, they often end up in homogeneous groups. Oftentimes, the impetus for such grouping is that they share common interests or characteristics, even if minor ones. This explains why, in the schools, the common sight in the cafeteria and the hallways is racial segregation of students. In the larger society, the same observation is common. Interestingly, the reason for such grouping may not necessarily be due to common interests as it is the quest for invisibility.

In all pluralistic societies, some form of blending is natural and is to be expected. Total assimilation into the dominant group, whereby an individual loses his or her identity, and homogeneous grouping, whereby individuals segregate from the dominant group, are both unhealthy to the larger interests of the society. A healthier alternative is a society where people are willing to learn about, and respect the ways of, each other. Although this is not easy to achieve, it is worth the attempt.

EDUCATIONAL IMPLICATIONS AND TIPS FOR PARENTS, TEACHERS, AND ADMINISTRATORS

According to the research, the observations made in this book are not surprising. The consequences, however, are not only significant in social, economic, and psychological terms but also lifelong terms. For example, when children are exposed to environments where they are always tokenized and have to look up to others for help in order to function or thrive, they are likely to grow up with compromised self-concept, self-esteem, and identity issues (Rice & Dolgin, 2005) and are likely to become followers, not leaders. For example, several studies indicate that African American youths have higher self-esteem when they are surrounded by others who share similar physical and social characteristics as themselves. However, their self-esteem decreases when they are exposed to societal prejudices (Martinez & Dukes, 1991; Comer, 1993; Dreyer, Jennings, Johnson, & Evans, 1994, as cited in Rice & Dolgin, 2005). All things being equal, this finding should hold true for other racial groups. Not surprisingly, disproportionately large numbers of black leaders and high-level professionals have been produced by historically black colleges and universities (HBCUs).

There are situations where individuals may develop significant physical and psychological—and even lethal—maladaptations to their token status. For example, some students have expressed the fact that as the minorities in specific situations, they not only felt that they were entering a hostile environment but also literally "felt sick to their stomach" each time they entered such environments. In the rare situations where the cognitive machineries of token individuals have been deranged, they may not only misbehave but do so in extreme ways. Take, for example, Cho Seung-Hui, the Korean-born immigrant who killed thirty-two people and injured twenty-nine students at Virginia Technical University. In an interview with Matt Apuzzo of Associated Press, some of Cho's high school classmates reported that he was so shy that he would never speak in class. At one time in class when he was forced to speak, he sounded as if he had something in his mouth—a situation that elicited laughter and racial slurs from some of his classmates, asking him to return to China, although he was Korean born. Of some interest is the fact that Cho wore sunglasses in classes (readers are encouraged to wonder why) and suffered from *selective mutism*, a rare psychological condition (normally in children) whereby individuals who are otherwise fully fluent in a language are rendered speechless in certain situations. Putatively, Cho's ostracism stems from his difference—both of his personhood (body) and speech—which in turn elicited responses from unwitting colleagues who behaved just like many people do: they exclude him, using a series of actions, reactions, and basic human behaviors. The outcome, however, is always the same: a feeling of isolation in the midst of crowds; a feeling of thirst even in the midst of many waters. Cho made frantic attempts to quench his thirst—unfortunately, by lethal means.

Cho's story is of interest because it is an estreme, rare case of more tolerable situations that inflict average people, as illustrated in some of the narratives in this book. The point being emphasized, however, is that humans—parents, teachers, administrators, and employers—need to be more conscious of the plight of individuals in tokenized situations and offer them necessary help. In the case of Cho, he had been referred to counseling services for help, but one can safely surmise that his token status contributed to his and many others' demise.

As emphasized in the last few sections, it is possible to help conscious minorities to become more comfortable and therefore better positioned to perform optimally. This is generally done by creating a welcoming environment. Although this is largely a physical process where people in the dominant group may be physically inviting by offering a smile or welcoming salutations, a part of this comforting process is psychological. For example, an environment that reminds one of home (or is familiar) may help. (Remember that, even in otherwise unfamiliar church environments, familiar songs helped to assuage the anxieties of some of the participants in the narratives.) Therefore, in school, parents, teachers, and administrators should consider using both physical and psychological avenues to help their minority students.

Tips for Parents

For many parents, school placement is a nonissue, since children attend schools in the local housing district, where people share the same physical characteristics and other interests. The decision as to where their children would attend school is often made during their housing considerations. Indeed, the residential real estate axiom "Location, location, location" partly means that home buyers are paying a premium price for "better" school districts. For average, nonminority parents, this rule makes sense. For parents who have conscious-minority children, however, this axiom must be changed to "Purchase your home in an area that suits your child."

Parents who have conscious-minority children often find themselves in situations where they are forced to compromise on the school location and placement choices for their children. For most people, the commonsense option is to purchase a home in a location where home prices are rising, and the school district is considered "good." The question, however, is "What defines what is 'good' for you?" For parents who have conscious-minority children, the first rule of thumb should be "Is my child going to be the acute minority, and do we have the means to address the consequences?" If the answer is no, then you may need to consider a different school district for your child. One suggestion is to make a comparative chart of merits and demerits of potential school districts. On your list, include the following items, in the same order of importance: (1) diversity of students; (2) academic performance of the schools; and (3) diversity of, and sensitivity of, teachers and administrators to diversity matters. What this means is that parents should be willing to consider a slightly less academic but more diverse school, but be willing to complement their children's academic work at home. In a pluralistic society, schools with the three components noted earlier have the potential to offer your child the best academic and social education, elements of what may be considered a "well-rounded" education.

For many parents, the die is already cast, and their children are already the minorities in their schools. The question then becomes "What can we do in order to address the consequences of my child's minority status?" Here are some suggestions for consideration:

- *Be proactive in your placement decisions.* If there are just a few minorities at the grade level, ask the administrators to consider placing at least two or more minorities (first, by the same physical characteristics, and second, by other characteristics). This helps dilute your child's token status in the same learning environment. If your child is clearly disadvantaged because of his or her minority status, consider moving your child to a magnet or charter school, if you have the means to do so. Remember that in some cases, you may need to provide your own transportation for your child. (There are often car-pooling opportunities in such schools.)
- *Be aware of your child's social life in school.* Ask your child's teacher about your child's social life in school. Visit the school several times, at different times of day, and randomly (e.g., before school, during break time, lunch time, right at dismissal), stand afar, and watch how your child is functioning socially in the school. Ask to sit in your child's class (in the back) and watch his or her performance in class. Chat with your child to find out what is going on in school (you need to be persistent: "I don't know" or "Nothing happened in school today" should not be acceptable). All these sources of information will give you ideas about the topics to discuss with the teachers.
- *Be visible, and encourage the invitation of role models.* If your child is a minority in school, he or she would be well-served by being more visible in the schools and making your child's psychological-intellectual needs known to teachers. All children need advocates. Children who are confident through circumstance (because they are in the majority) and are therefore more vocal often *appear* smart to teachers (an issue of perception and impressions), and they may have their ideas tested out for correction. Minority children

who are trying to become invisible need the voices of their parents in order for their gifts to become known to teachers. Another important idea is to encourage teachers to invite diverse guests into the school—to read in class, give talks and demonstrations, in support of the curriculum.

- *Add to the school curriculum.* Many teachers are often aware of diversity among students. However, because the idea of "diversity" can be defined in so many different ways, your child's teacher may not be aware that your child may have a specific need—especially intellectual needs. You need to fill that gap. Consider donating books or other materials that reflect your child's needs or heroes. A nice, large poster of a cultural hero in the classroom for the whole year goes a long way to create a "presence" that may boost your child's self-concept. Another important idea is to follow your child's curriculum, ask questions, and make corrections to self-esteem-damaging impressions or misconceptions your child may develop as a result of lessons—especially in social studies. For example, historical information is being rewritten (in newer books) from new, more accurate, and multiple perspectives that better represent the voices of a pluralistic society. Therefore, you will need to educate yourself about the vast amount of information that is often not taught as a part of the school curriculum.
- *Promote your child's self-esteem.* If your child is struggling with self-esteem issues in school, it is possible that your child will sometimes arrive home a bit irritable (or grouchy). Understand his or her situation by offering a willing ear and understanding. Look for and create opportunities for small successes, and offer praise to boost his or her self-esteem.
- *Create inclusive social settings for your child.* Since your child may be lacking a diverse environment in school—with the potential of affecting his or her self-esteem—consider creating a healthier social system for your child. This may include inviting your child's schoolmates to play outside school, thus fostering the creation of new friends. Consider options where your child will meet others who are like him- or herself for identity recentering. Local YMCAs, sport teams, and churches are a good start.
- *Create positive images at home.* For children who are physically different from their schoolmates, one of the most important actions parents can take is to passively (i.e., unbeknownst to them) surround them with home environments that are saturated with images that look like themselves. Consider

watching movies with such heroes, and offer helpful books, posters, and other decorations as "incidental gifts." Discourage your children from watching images (including "classic" movies) that cast people like themselves in inferior roles or subservient to others. Allow them enough time to grow and develop their own sense of identity before saddling them with the extra burden of mental subjugation.

Tips for Administrators

In a pluralistic society, school administrators and teachers may rightly acknowledge the value of diversity. Therefore, although they may notice the presence of minorities (or diversity) in the school, they would, at best, be passive in their classroom placements. This is often done in order to ensure fairness. Based on our findings, however, passive placement of students can result in situations where students can become disadvantaged. School administrators and teachers should therefore consider "active placement" of minorities, as already noted.

The second issue has to do with the specific teacher in whose class to place the minority student. Teachers who are not only exposed to, but are sensitive to, diversity issues are better candidates for minority students' placement. For example, the teacher who is very interested in Bolivia and has previously traveled there is likely to be excited about, and take interest in, the Bolivian student and is more likely to address his or her needs. Obviously, teachers who are kind but firm are better candidates for minority student placement.

Tips for Teachers

Different instructional strategies produce different learning outcomes. Learning outcomes can be either content related or skill development related, an example of which is to appreciate and respect others. In the context of teaching minority learners, inclusive instructional strategies are of paramount interest because they have the added advantage of fostering skill development as a learning outcome. A few ideas are suggested here:

- Implement the applicable ideas found in the parent and administrators sections.
- Use cooperative learning strategies to include all learners. Teach your students about the notion of "cooperativity."

- When grouping students, use intentional, grouping dynamics to include all learners. For example, you may use specific selection criteria to actively create groups that generate certain behavioral outcomes.
- Until your minority student feels a part of the class and truly included, consider creating the groups, since they are likely to pick their friends first.
- Change your groups, as needed, especially if your minority student is not yet comfortable. Changing groups also helps students to learn from new perspectives.
- Be careful not to single out the minority student as the specialist on what characterizes him or her. For example, do not ask the blind student all the questions about eyes—unless you have prediscussed it and can use it to enhance his or her self-esteem.

CONCLUDING REFLECTIONS

In conclusion, the *minority effect* is a raw, human experience that can be characterized as a quest for comfort, acceptance, or invisibility and one that often leads to a set of mostly negative behaviors. On occasion, however, it can stimulate or force individuals to perform beyond their conventional limits. People who are the conscious minorities are self-conscious individuals who may view themselves as intruders in an environment that is ready to reject them. They look around and wonder if, and what, people are thinking about them. Worst of all, it is often not what others do to them but what they do to themselves that create their anxieties. In some cases, because they feel like intruders, conscious minorities may find ways to prove to their imaginary audience that they have the right to be there—as if they need to earn their presence in that environment. Yet, being humans, this process often becomes too heavy a burden to bear. The result is a feeling of inferiority and a behavior that is abnormal. Fortunately, the narratives in this book illustrate that humans have the capacity to promote, discourage, or be passive in other people's comfort-seeking processes. Perhaps one lesson we can learn is that humans can take advantage of the same machinery—of human responsiveness to certain stimuli, especially "comforting stimuli," such as smiles and generosity—in order to create a better world for all humans, both the majority and the minority. In schools and workplaces, parents, teachers, administrators, and employers have the opportunity to use the same human mechanisms to ensure that the needs of their conscious minorities are addressed sufficiently.

Vincent van Gogh, the Dutch impressionist painter, noted, "I dream my painting, and then I paint my dream." Perhaps, as humans, we create our own realities and live them; and for conscious minorities, a world of anxiety is created for, and by, themselves. François Jacob once wondered, "How is it that, in the human body, reproduction is the only function to be performed by an organ of which an individual carries only one half so that he has to spend an enormous amount of time to find another half?" A corollary question is, Why is it that humans, for all our complexities and sophistication, feel incomplete and unfulfilled, unless we are accepted by others? To such questions, Van Gogh might respond, "One may have a blazing hearth in one's soul and yet no one ever comes to sit by it. Passersby see only a wisp of smoke from the chimney and continue on the way." Through all the anxieties of all humanity, as illustrated in this book, it takes often the hand of a single individual to quench the yearnings of the human soul; in a world of needless strife and misunderstanding, we can see the potential power of one—anybody in the dominant group—to make another human comfortable. Perhaps, as partakers of a common earth, we need to learn more about the nature of humanity in order to embrace our expression and need for comfort—comfort that can only be granted by the *other*. Yet again, perhaps, there are outstretched hands that are invisible to us, because we have been blinded by our own prejudices. Here's an invitation to sight!

SUGGESTED QUESTIONS FOR DISCUSSION

1. When were you the minority in a given context?
2. In what ways would you consider President Barak Obama and Senator Hillary Clinton as national cases of the minority experience?
3. In what ways were presidential candidates Barak Obama and Hillary Clinton treated like minorities? What are some of the mechanisms they used to try to overcome their minority experiences?
4. What are some of the possible causes, reasons, or origins of the anxiety that is associated with the minority experience? Is this anxiety a figment of people's own imaginations or creations, or is it the result of something society inculcates in its citizens?
5. The notion of "conscious minority" is partly an issue of self-judgment. Why is it that tokenized individuals unconsciously judge (or assess)

themselves (and therefore become anxious), even when others are not judging them?

6. Which case stories in the book stood out for you and why?
7. What were some of the surprising pieces of information you found in the book?
8. Describe experiences in your own life where some of the narratives in the book connected with your experiences.
9. In what ways do these case stories help you to understand the plight of situational minority students in your school or workplace?
10. Describe five things you can do to minimize the effects of the minority experience for others.
11. What are some of the dysfunctional behavioral consequences of the minority experience?
12. What are the more appropriate ways to respond to the dysfunctional behaviors you have described?

Bibliography

Akbar, N. (1998). *Know thy self.* Tallahassee, FL: Mind Productions.

Apple, M. (1996). *Cultural politics and education.* New York: Teachers College Press.

Apuzzo, M. (2007, April 20). Ex-classmates: Cho was painfully shy, ostracized: Schoolboy was bullied, but didn't respond when others reached out." *Charlotte Observer,* p. 5A.

Banks, J. A. (1988). Ethnicity, class, cognitive, and motivational styles: Research and teaching implications. In J. Kretovics & E. J. Nussel (Eds.), *Transforming urban education* (pp. 277–290). Boston: Allyn & Bacon.

Banks, J. A. (2005). Multicultural education: Characteristics and goals. In J. A. Banks & C. A. M. Banks (Eds.), *Multicultural education* (pp. 3–30). Hoboken, NJ: Wiley Jossey-Bass.

Boykin, A. W. (2001). The challenges of cultural socialization in the schooling of African American elementary school children: Exposing the hidden curriculum. In W. Watkins, J. Lewis, & V. Chou (Eds.), *Race and education.* Boston: Allyn & Bacon.

Comer, J. (1993). *African-American parents and child development: An agenda for school success.* Paper presented at the biannual meetings of the Society for Research in Child Development, New Orleans.

Cross, W. E. (1978). The Thomas and Cross models of psychological nigrescence: A review. *Journal of Black Psychology, 5,* 13–31.

Cross, W. E. (1991). *Shades of black: Diversity in African American identity.* Philadelphia: Temple University Press.

Cummins, J. (1996). *Negotiating identities: Education for empowerment in a diverse society.* Ontario, CA: California Association for Bilingual Education.

Dei, G. J., Mazzuca, J., McIsaac, E., & Zine, J. (1997). *Reconstructing "dropout": A critical ethnography of the dynamics of black students' disengagement from school.* Toronto: University of Toronto Press.

Delgado, R., & Stefancic, J. (Eds.). (1997). *Critical white studies: Looking behind the mirror.* Philadelphia: Temple University Press.

DeVito, J. A. (2004). *The interpersonal communication book* (10th ed.). Boston: Allyn & Bacon.

Dewey, J. (1916). *Democracy and education.* New York: Free Press.

Dreyer, T. H., Jennings, C., Johnson, F., & Evans, D. (1994). *Culture and personality in urban schools: Identity status, self-concepts, and loss of control among high school students and monolingual and bilingual homes.* Paper presented at the meeting of the Society for Research on Adolescents, San Diego.

DuBois, W. E. B. (1903). *The souls of black folk.* Chicago: McClurg.

Erickson, F. (2005). Culture in society and in educational practices. In J. A. Banks & C. A. M. Banks (Eds.), *Multicultural education* (pp. 31–60). Hoboken, NJ: Wiley Jossey-Bass.

Evans-Winters, V. E. (2005). *Teaching black girls resiliency in urban classrooms.* New York: Lang.

Ferguson, A. A. (2000). *Bad boys: Public schools in the making of black masculinity.* Ann Arbor: University of Michigan Press.

Freire, P. (1993/2000). *Pedagogy of the oppressed.* New York: Continuum. (Original work published 1970.)

Gay, G. (2000). *Culturally responsive teaching: Theory, research, and practice.* New York: Teachers College Press.

Giroux, H. A. (1997). *Pedagogy and the politics of hope: Theory, culture, and schooling: A Critical reader.* Boulder, CO: Westview Press.

Graves, T. D. (1967). Psychological acculturation in a tri-ethnic community. *South-Western Journal of Anthropology, 23,* 337–350.

Gruenert, S. (2005). Correlations of collaborative school cultures with student achievement. *Urban Education, 89*(645), 43–55.

Gudykunst, W. B., & Ting-Toomey, S. (1988). *Culture and interpersonal communication.* Newbury Park, CA: Sage.

Guy, T. (1999). Culture as context for adult education: The need for culturally relevant adult education. *New Directions for Adult and Continuing Education, 82,* 5–17.

Haberman, M. (1991). The pedagogy of poverty versus good teaching. *Phi Delta Kappan, 73*(4), 290–294.

Hayes, R. L., & Lin, H. (1994). Coming to America: Developing social support systems for international students, *Journal of Multicultural Counseling and Development, 22*(1), 7–16.

Helms, J. E. (1984). Toward a theoretical explanation of the effects of race on counseling: An African American and white model. *Counseling Psychologist, 12*(4), 153–163.

Howard, G. R. (1999). *We can't teach what we don't know: White teachers, multiracial schools.* New York: Teachers College Press.

Howard, T. (2001). Powerful pedagogy for African American students. *Urban Education, 36*(2), 179–202.

Hutchison, C. B. *Teaching diverse learners: Basic principles, classroom insights, and best practices.* Unpublished manuscript.

Irvine, J. J. (1990). *Black students and school failure: Policies, practices, and prescriptions.* Westport, CT: Greenwood.

Ladson-Billings, G. (1992). Culturally relevant teaching: The key to making multicultural education work. In C. Grant (Ed.), *Research and multicultural education: From the margin to the mainstream* (pp. 106–121). London: Falmer Press.

Latham, N. (1999). The teacher-student mismatch. *Educational Leadership, 56*(7), 84–85.

Martinez, R., & Dukes, R. L. (1991). Ethnic and gender differences and self-esteem. *Youth and Society, 3,* 318–338.

Ogbu, J. (1991). Minority coping responses and school experience. *Journal of Psychohistory, 18,* 433–456.

Ogbu, J., & Fordham, S. (1986). Black students' school success: Coping with the "burden of 'acting white.'" *Urban Review, 18,* 176–206.

Osborne, J. W. (2001). Testing stereotype threat: Does anxiety explain race and sex differences in achievement? *Contemporary Educational Psychology, 26,* 291–310.

Pedersen, P. B. (1991). Counseling international students. *Counseling Psychologist, 19*(1), 10–58.

Rice, F. P., & Dolgin, K. G. (2005). *The adolescent: Development, relationships, and culture.* Boston: Allyn and Bacon.

Saenz, D. S. (1994). Token status and problem-solving deficits: Detrimental effects of distinctiveness and performance monitoring. *Social Cognition, 12,* 61–74.

Simmons, R. G., Brown, L., Bush, D. M., & Blyth, D. A. (1978). Self-esteem and achievement of black and white adolescents. *Social Problems, 26,* 86–96.

Somé, M. P. (1998). *The healing wisdom of Africa: Finding life purpose through nature, ritual, and community.* New York: Penguin Putnam.

Steele, C. M. (1999). Thin ice: Stereotype threat and black college students. *Atlantic Monthly, 284*(2), 44–54.

Traore, R. (2006). Voices of African students in America: "We're not from the jungle." *Multicultural Perspectives, 8*(2), 29–34.

Traore, R., & Lukens, R. J. (2006). *"This isn't the America I thought I'd find": African students in the urban U.S. high school.* Lanham, MD: University Press of America.

Villegas, A. (1988). School failure and cultural mismatch: Another view. *Urban Review, 20*(4), 253–265.

Villegas, A., & Lucas, T. (2002). *Educating culturally responsive teachers: A coherent approach.* Albany: State University of New York Press.

Ware, F. (2006). Warm demander pedagogy. *Urban Education, 41* (4), 427–456.

Winfield, L. (1986). Teacher beliefs toward academically at-risk students in inner urban schools. *Urban Review, 18*(4), 253–267.

Woodson, C. G. (1933/2000). *The mis-education of the Negro.* Chicago: Associated Publishers.

About the Editor and Contributors

Charles B. Hutchison teaches at the University of North Carolina at Charlotte and was a classroom teacher for twelve years. He is the author of the book *Teaching in America: A Cross-Cultural Guide for International Teachers and Their Employers* (Springer, 2005) and the forthcoming books *Teaching Diverse Learners with Basic Principles, Classroom Insights, and Best Practices* (Allyn and Bacon) and *Global Issues in Education: Pedagogy, Policy, School Practices, and the Minority Experience* (coedited with Greg Wiggan; Rowman and Littlefield). He is the recipient of Recognition and Key to the City of Boston. He has been featured in local and international news media, including CBS *NightWatch*, Voice of America, the *Boston Globe*, the *Washington Post*, and several others. His articles have appeared in several journals, including *Phi Delta Kappan*, *Intercultural Education*, *Cultural Studies of Science Education*, and *School Science and Mathematics*. He has lived and worked in Africa, Europe, and the United States. His research interests include cultural cognition, international, diversity, and cross-cultural issues in education. He can be reached at chutchis@uncc.edu.

Maria Abelquist is a graduate of Berea College and is pursuing her master of arts in teaching at the University of North Carolina at Charlotte (UNC-Charlotte). She specializes in teaching language arts to middle school students.

Tiffany Adams is a second grade instructor with the Charlotte-Mecklenburg schools in Charlotte, North Carolina and is pursuing a post-baccalaureate certificate in teaching at UNC-Charlotte.

Clifford Afam was formerly a nursing instructor at Stanly Community College at Albemarle and is currently the director of a healthcare facility and education consultant at Divine Health Academy College of Health Sciences at Charlotte.

Daniel Blanton was formerly a civil engineer and a U.S. Army veteran of eight years. He currently teaches Algebra I at Kings Mountain High School, North Carolina and is pursuing a post-baccalaureate certificate in teaching at UNC-Charlotte.

Brian Bongiovanni is pursuing a post-baccalaureate certificate in teaching at UNC-Charlotte.

Carletta Bradley is a public high school choral arts teacher with Union County schools in North Carolina and is pursuing a post-baccalaureate certificate in teaching at UNC-Charlotte.

Winfree Spears Brisley graduated from UNC-Chapel Hill with a BA in political science and is completing her graduate certificate in middle grades education at UNC-Charlotte.

Tracie S. Clark, a former communication instructor at the University of Maryland-College Park, currently teaches communication courses at Central Piedmont Community College.

David W. Cornett is an undergraduate student at the College of Education, UNC-Charlotte.

Jim Cross left a twenty-year career in the restaurant industry to become a lateral-entry teacher. He teaches algebra at Hopewell High School in Charlotte, North Carolina.

Betty Danzi was formerly a technology consultant and is currently pursuing a teaching certificate in secondary mathematics at UNC-Charlotte.

Arron Deckard is an undergraduate student at the College of Education, UNC-Charlotte.

Ryan Delehant is pursuing a post-baccalaureate certificate in teaching at UNC-Charlotte.

Joseph Edmonds is a Fellow of the Society of Actuaries and an Enrolled Actuary. He holds two master's degrees in mathematics and economics and has consulting practice in Charlotte, North Carolina.

Lauren Emerson is pursuing a post-baccalaureate certificate in teaching at UNC-Charlotte.

Angela Jakeway is an instructor of German at UNC-Charlotte.

LaTasha Jones was a middle school teacher in Atlanta and currently teaches middle grades education and multicultural courses at Valdosta State University.

Stephanie Johnston is an English teacher at West Rowan High School in Mount Ulla, North Carolina, and is completing her master's degree in English education at UNC-Charlotte.

Kalilah Kirkpatrick is an eighth grade language arts teacher in Charlotte, North Carolina.

Karlie Kissman is pursuing a post-baccalaureate certificate in teaching at UNC-Charlotte.

Jeremy Laliberte is pursuing a post-baccalaureate certificate in teaching at UNC-Charlotte.

Melissa Loftis is a second grade elementary school teacher in Charlotte, North Carolina, and is finishing her master's degree in teaching English as a second language.

Lisa McCrimmon is pursuing a post-baccalaureate certificate in teaching at UNC-Charlotte.

Anita McGee is pursuing a post-baccalaureate certificate in teaching at UNC-Charlotte.

Aja' Pharr is pursuing a post-baccalaureate certificate in teaching at UNC-Charlotte.

Matthew Reid taught at Troutman Elementary School and is currently teaching humanities at the Northview International Baccalaureate School in Statesville, North Carolina.

Crystal Sisk is an undergraduate student at the College of Education, UNC-Charlotte.

Loretta Sullivan graduated from Florida State University and has recently become licensed to teach high school English through UNC-Charlotte's post-baccalaureate program.

Ora Uhuru is pursuing a post-baccalaureate certificate in teaching at UNC-Charlotte.

Ann Wright recently received her teaching license in middle grades language arts from UNC-Charlotte.

Breinigsville, PA USA
29 April 2010
237021BV00003B/8/P

9 781607 093947